FRANK BRIDG

Four Pieces
for cello and piano

Edited by
Julian Lloyd Webber

FABER *ff* MUSIC

CELLO

BERCEUSE
1901

Edited by Julian Lloyd Webber

FRANK BRIDGE
(1879—1941)

SERENADE

1903

ÉLÉGIE
1904

CRADLE SONG
1910

FRANK BRIDGE

Four Pieces
for cello and piano

Edited by
Julian Lloyd Webber

FABER *ff* MUSIC

These four pieces were composed separately between the years 1901 and 1910 and appeared in print in several different versions, ranging from piano solo to full orchestra. They were all originally written, however, for cello and piano. The editor has been responsible for the addition of bowings and fingerings.

FIRST PUBLICATION

Berceuse: 1902 by Keith Prowse Ltd. *Serenade*: 1906 by Reid Bros Ltd.
Elégie: 1911 by Goodwin and Tabb Ltd. *Cradle Song*: 1911 by Goodwin and Tabb Ltd.

DURATIONS

Berceuse: $2^1/_2$ mins. *Serenade*: 2 mins.
Elégie: 3 mins. *Cradle Song*: 2 mins.

© 1982 by Faber Music Ltd
This edition first published in 1982 by Faber Music Ltd
3 Queen Square London WC1N 3AU
Cover design by S & M Tucker
Printed in England by Caligraving Ltd
All rights reserved
ISBN 0-571-50626-7

To buy Faber Music publications or to find out about the full range of titles available
please contact your local music retailer or Faber Music sales enquiries:

Faber Music Limited, Burnt Mill, Elizabeth Way, Harlow, CM20 2HX England
Tel: +44 (0)1279 82 89 82 Fax: +44 (0)1279 82 89 83
sales@fabermusic.com www.fabermusic.com

BERCEUSE
1901

Edited by Julian Lloyd Webber

FRANK BRIDGE
(1879–1941)

SERENADE
1903

ÉLÉGIE

1904

to Phyllis Compton

CRADLE SONG

1910

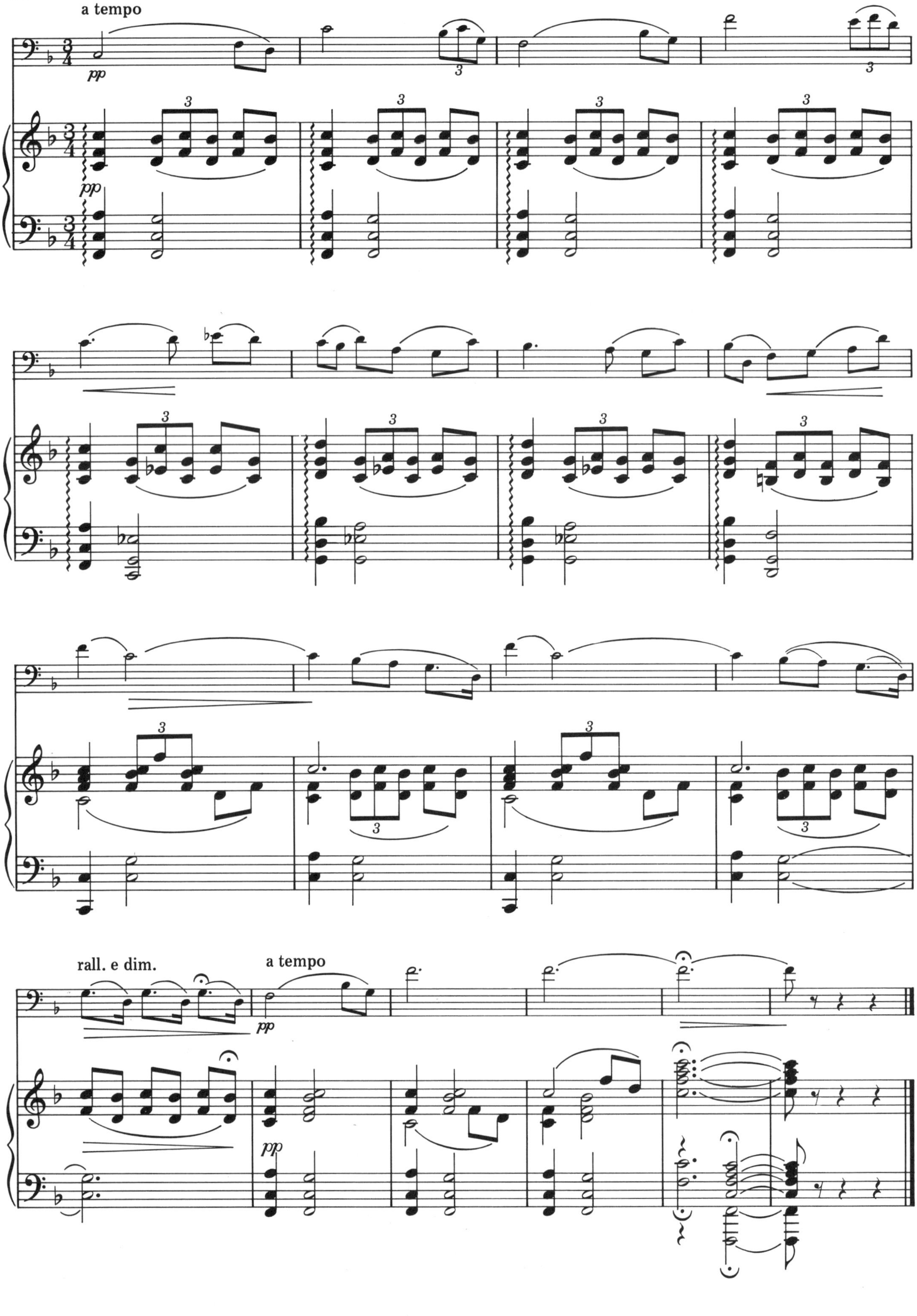
a tempo
pp
pp
rall. e dim.
a tempo
pp
pp

NON-VERBAL REASONING

PRACTICE TEST PAPERS

Book 1

11+

NON-VERBAL REASONING

FOR GL ASSESSMENT

4 MULTIPLE CHOICE PRACTICE TEST PAPERS

11+

Pamela Macey

Introduction

The tests

These tests have been written to provide your child with an opportunity to practise a formal type of examination paper before taking the actual exam for school selection at age eleven. Both the content and the layout are very similar to that which will be used in those exams, although the level of difficulty may not be exactly the same. The scores that your child gets with these practice papers will provide you with an indication of their level of achievement, but cannot be guaranteed as an indicator of their actual performance in the exam as there are other factors that affect the outcome, such as the overall standard of all the candidates. These papers will, however, help your child to prepare and develop skills to enable them to approach the actual test confidently and to achieve the best that they can.

Getting ready for the tests

Agree with your child a good time to take the practice papers. This should be when they are fresh and alert. You also need to find a good place to work, a place that is comfortable and free from distractions. Being able to see a clock is helpful as they learn how to pace themselves.

Take some time talking with your child before they take the tests, so that they understand the purpose of the practice papers and how doing them will help them to prepare for the actual exam. Explain how they may find some parts easy and others more challenging, but that they need to have a go at every question. If they 'get stuck' on a question they should just mark it with an asterisk and carry on. At the end of the paper they may have time to go back and try again. If not, after completing the paper you can look at those questions together.

Administering the tests

Multiple-choice tests

For this style of test, the answers are recorded on a separate answer sheet. The answer sheet will be marked by a computer in the actual exam, so it is important that it is used correctly. Practising now with an answer sheet will reduce the chance of your child getting anxious or confused during the actual test.

Answers are indicated by drawing a clear pencil line through the appropriate box. It is very important that answers are marked clearly with a line through the answer box and that there are no other marks. If your child indicates one answer and then wants to change their response, the first mark must be fully rubbed out. This process may not seem necessary for the practice paper, but familiarisation with the answer sheet format will be a great help for your child in the real exam. For this practice paper there is no need for your child to complete the sections such as 'School No.' or 'Pupil No.' – these will only be required in the actual exam.

The test questions

These tests are made up of five separate sections, with instructions, an example and some practice questions at the beginning of each section, followed by twelve questions. In the actual exam each section would be administered and timed separately, with the invigilator reading out the instructions, checking the practice questions and then timing the section. For the purposes of practising however, the papers can be used in different ways, and three options are set out below:

OPTION 1: Open the test booklet with your child and read through the instructions together. Get them to do the practice question and then check the answer key, before allowing six minutes for the following twelve questions. If they have not finished the section in the time, make a mark by the question they are on and then complete the section. When marking the test later, you will be able to see how many questions would have been answered correctly in the time available and if further practice is needed to increase their speed of working. Repeat this process for the other four sections.

OPTION 2: Ask your child to read through the instructions and the example at the beginning of the first section themselves, and then do the practice question with you providing the answer from the answer key. When they are ready, you should then time them to do the next twelve questions, allowing six minutes. If they have not finished the section in the time, make a mark by the question they are on and then complete the section. When marking the test later, you will be able to see how many questions would have been answered correctly in the time available and if further practice is needed to increase their speed of working. Repeat this process for the other four sections.

OPTION 3: You can simply give the practice paper to your child and get them to read the instructions and to work through the paper in their own time, without any help or checking from you. In this case they will need to be told to ignore the instruction 'Wait until you are told to go on' written in the papers. There would not be any opportunity to check answers to the practice questions while working through the paper.

All of these options will provide your child with practice. Option 1 is the closest to the real exam that they will take, and as working at the right speed can be difficult for some children, options 2 and 3 will help you to both identify and practise working at an appropriate speed.

Contents

Non-Verbal Reasoning
Multiple-Choice
Practice Test A

Read these instructions carefully:

1. You must not open or turn over this booklet until you are told to do so.

2. The booklet contains a multiple-choice test, in which you have to mark your answer to each question on the separate answer sheet.

3. There are five sections in this test. Each section starts with an explanation of what to do, followed by one or two examples with the answer marked on the answer sheet. You will then be asked to do some practice questions.

4. You should mark only one answer for each question.

5. Make sure that you draw a firm line clearly through the rectangle next to your answer. Rub out any mistakes as well as you can and put in your new answer.

6. Complete the questions as quickly and carefully as you can. If you find that you cannot do a question, do not waste time on it, go on to the next one.

7. You may do any rough working on a separate sheet of paper.

Section 1

In each of the questions below, there is a sequence of squares with one square left empty. Look at the five squares on the right and find the one that should take the place of the empty square to complete the sequence. Mark it on your answer sheet.

Here is an example to help you.

Example

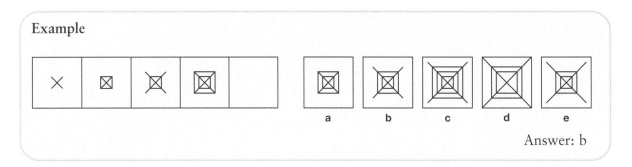

Answer: b

Now try these practice questions.

P1.

P2.

WAIT UNTIL YOU ARE TOLD TO GO ON

1.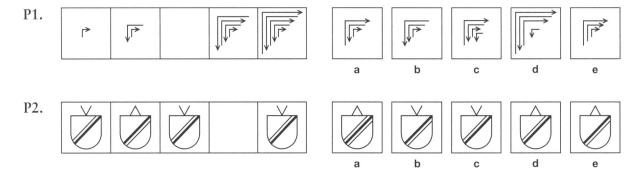

2.

3.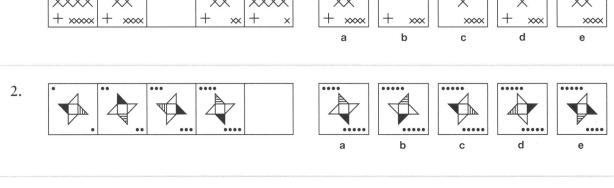

4.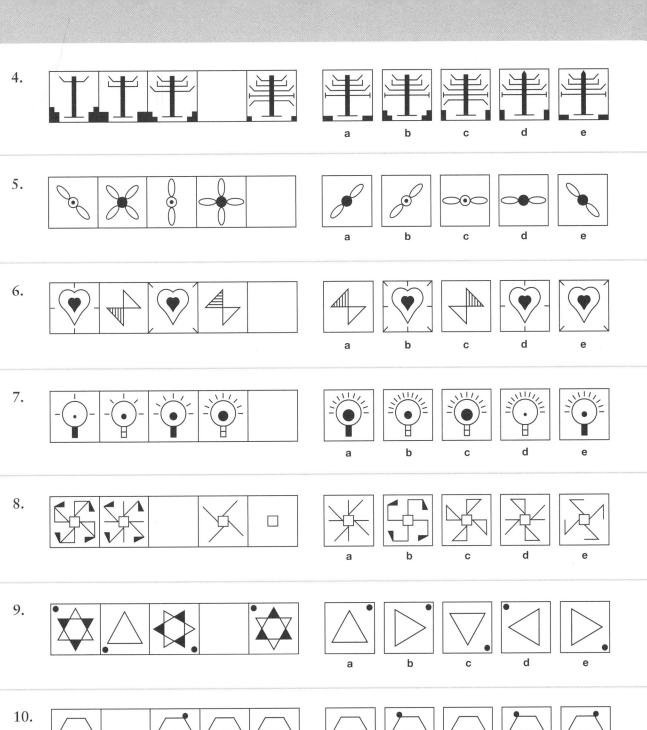

5.

6.

7.

8.

9.

10.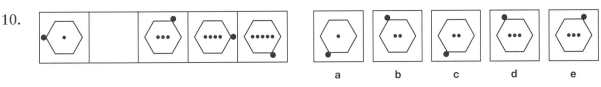

11.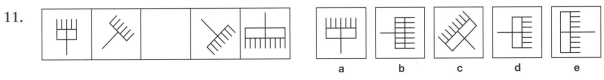

12.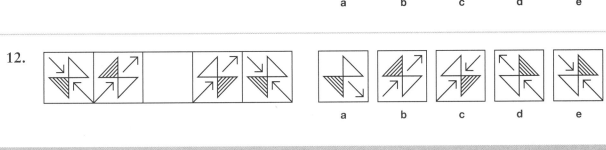

Section 2

In each question below, there are two shapes or patterns on the left which are similar in some way. Decide how they are similar. Find which of the five shapes on the right is most like the two shapes. Mark it on the answer sheet.

Here is an example to help you.

Example

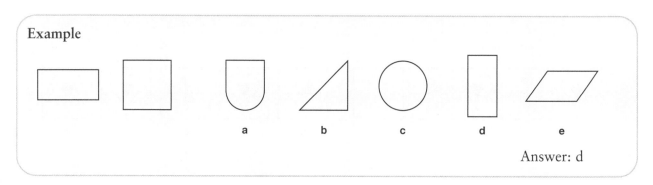

Answer: d

Now try these practice questions.

P1.

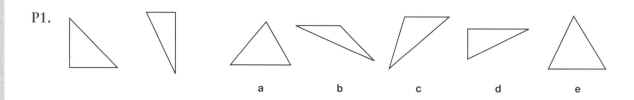

P2.

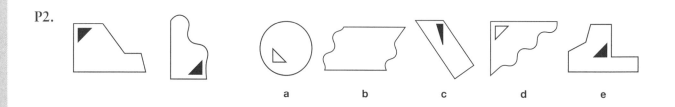

P3.

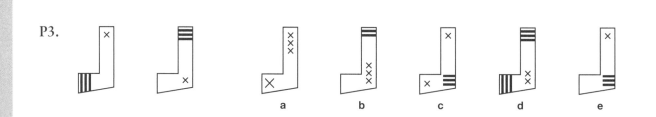

WAIT UNTIL YOU ARE TOLD TO GO ON

1.
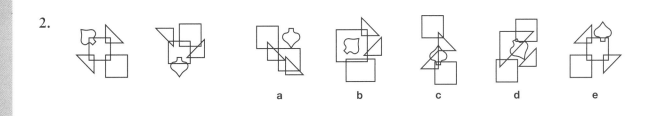

                a   b   c   d   e

2.
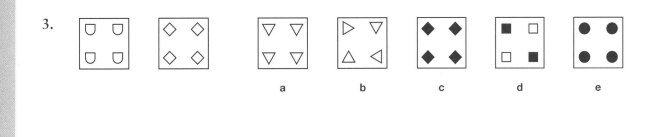

                a   b   c   d   e

3.
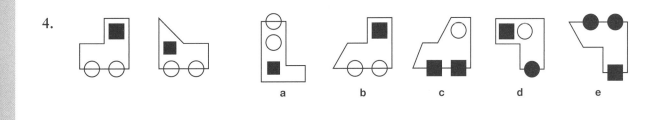

                a   b   c   d   e

4.
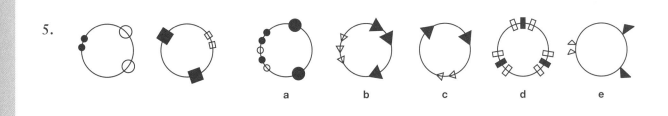

                a   b   c   d   e

5.
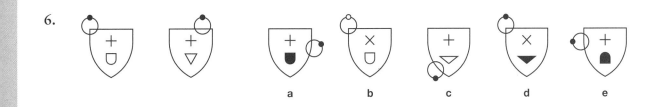

                a   b   c   d   e

6.

                a   b   c   d   e

7.

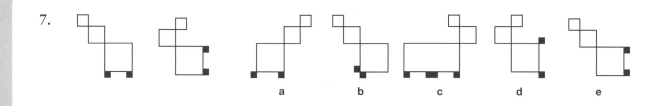

       a   b   c   d   e

8.

       a   b   c   d   e

9.

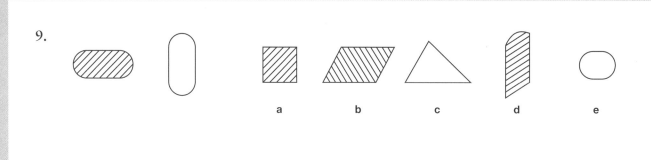

       a   b   c   d   e

10.

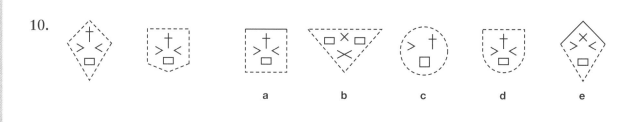

       a   b   c   d   e

11.

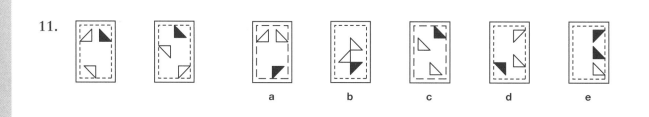

       a   b   c   d   e

12.

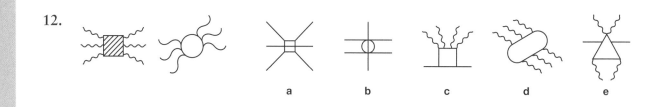

       a   b   c   d   e

Section 3

In each of the questions below, there are two shapes on the left with an arrow between them. Look at them carefully and decide how the second shape is related to the first shape. There is then a third shape and another arrow followed by five more shapes. Decide which of the five shapes completes the second pair in the same way as the first pair. Mark it on your answer sheet.

Here is an example to help you.

Example

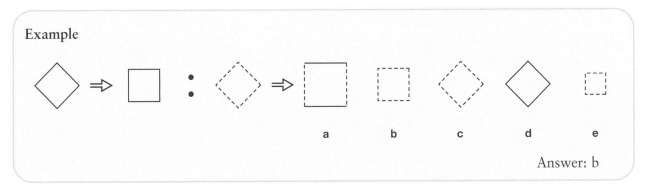

a   b   c   d   e

Answer: b

Now try these practice questions.

P1.

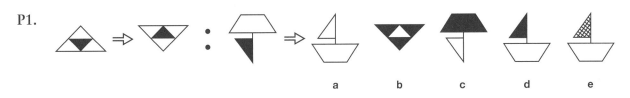

a   b   c   d   e

P2.

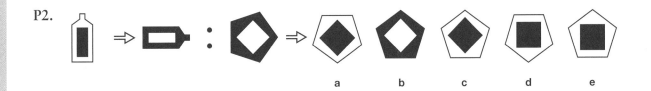

a   b   c   d   e

WAIT UNTIL YOU ARE TOLD TO GO ON

1.

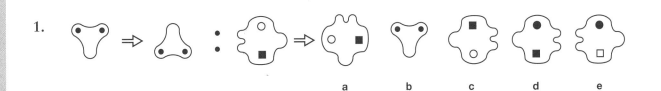

a   b   c   d   e

2.

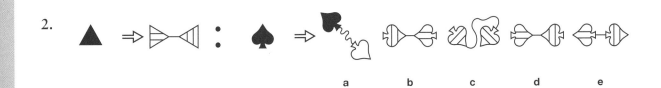

a   b   c   d   e

NOW GO ON TO THE NEXT PAGE

3.

a   b   c   d   e

4.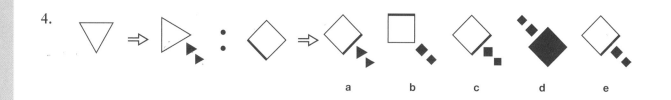

a   b   c   d   e

5.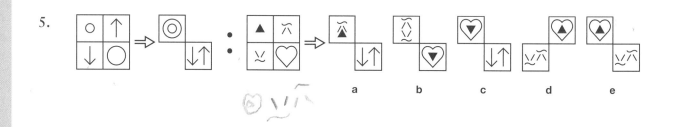

a   b   c   d   e

6.

a   b   c   d   e

7.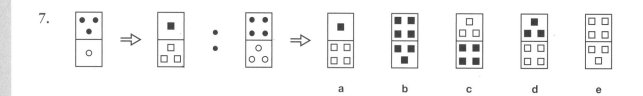

a   b   c   d   e

8.

a   b   c   d   e

9.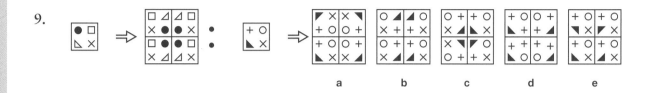

a   b   c   d   e

10.

a   b   c   d   e

11.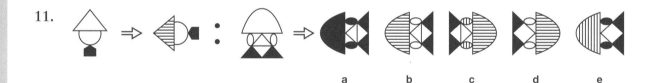

a   b   c   d   e

12.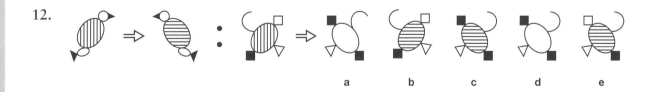

a   b   c   d   e

Section 4

In the grids below, one square has been left empty. Look carefully at the five squares to the right and select the square that should complete the grid. Mark it on your answer sheet.

Here is an example to help you.

Example

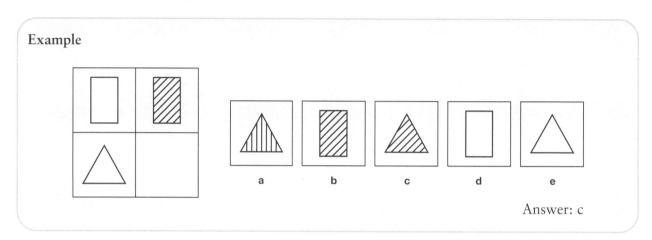

Answer: c

Now try these practice questions.

P1.

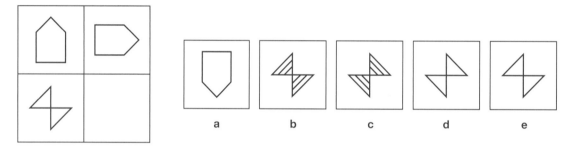

P2.

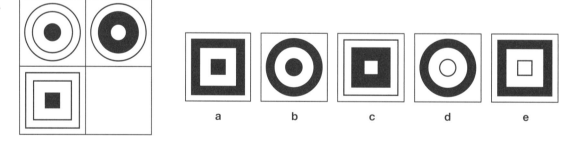

P3.

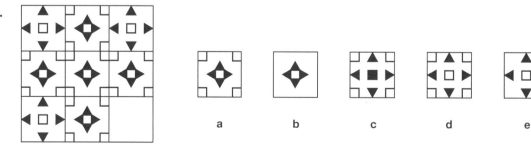

P4.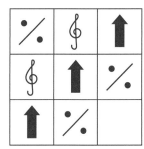

a   b   c   d   e

WAIT UNTIL YOU ARE TOLD TO GO ON

1.

a   b   c   d   e

2.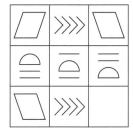

a   b   c   d   e

3.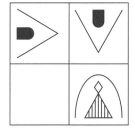

a   b   c   d   e

4.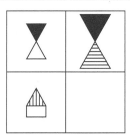

a   b   c   d   e

5.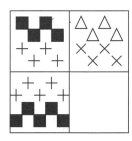

a   b   c   d   e

NOW GO ON TO THE NEXT PAGE

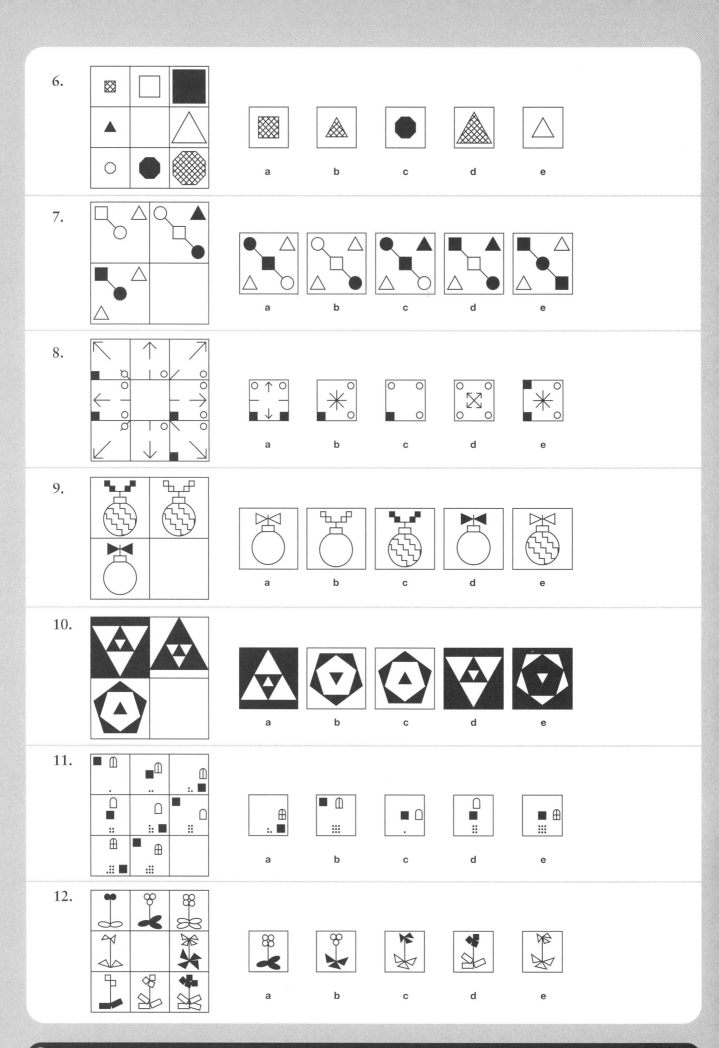

In the questions below, you have to work out a code. You are given some shapes and the codes that go with them. Decide how the codes match the shapes. Then look at the test shape and find its correct code from the five given on the right. Mark it on your answer sheet.

Here are two examples to help you.

Look at Example 1.

Example 1

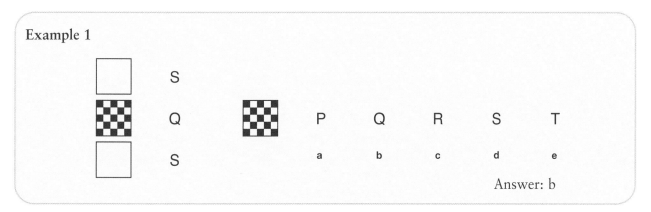

S stands for a white square and Q for a checked square, so the code for the test shape must be Q.

Now look at Example 2.

Example 2

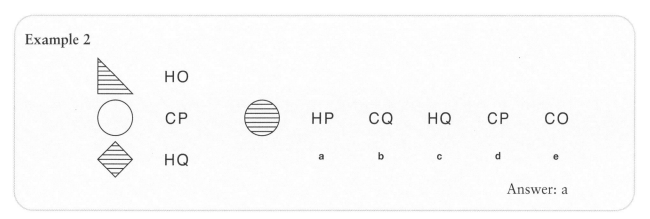

This time the shapes on the left have two letters. Find two shapes that have a letter in common. The first and the third shape both start with H, so H must be the code for shading. The second letter is different for each shape, so the second letter must be the code for shape. The test shape is a shaded circle, so its code is HP. HP is option *a*, so *a* is the correct answer.

Now try these practice questions.

P1.

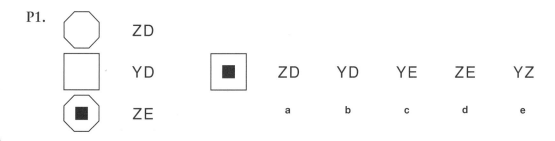

P2.

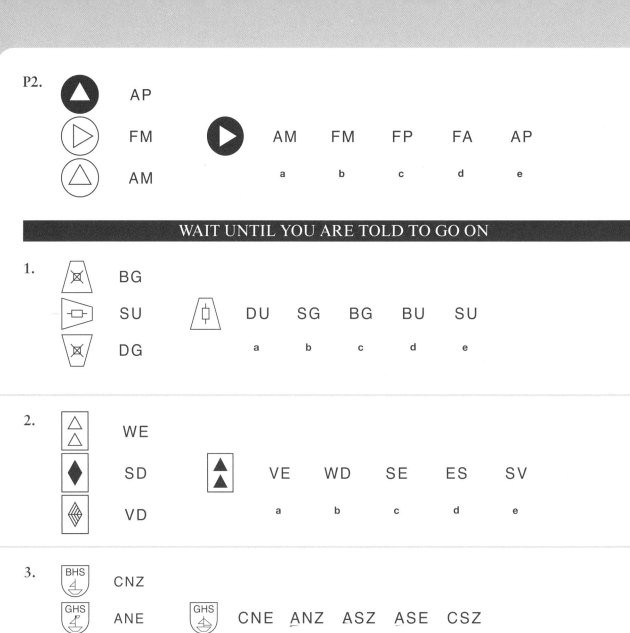

▲ (filled triangle in filled circle)	AP
▷ (triangle right in circle)	FM
△ (triangle in circle)	AM

▶   AM   FM   FP   FA   AP

     a   b   c   d   e

WAIT UNTIL YOU ARE TOLD TO GO ON

1.

BG

SU

DG

DU   SG   BG   BU   SU

 a   b   c   d   e

2.

WE

SD

VD

VE   WD   SE   ES   SV

 a   b   c   d   e

3.

CNZ

ANE

CSE

CNE   ANZ   ASZ   ASE   CSZ

 a   b   c   d   e

4.

LWS

ENT

LNC

LNS   EWS   LWC   EWT   LWT

 a   b   c   d   e

5.

GT

BT

GD

BC

BT   GC   BD   GT   BC

 a   b   c   d   e

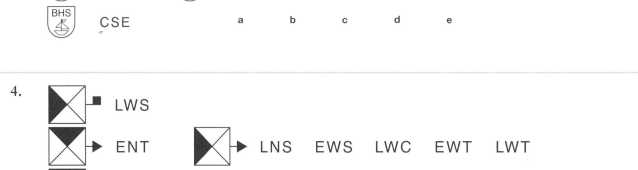

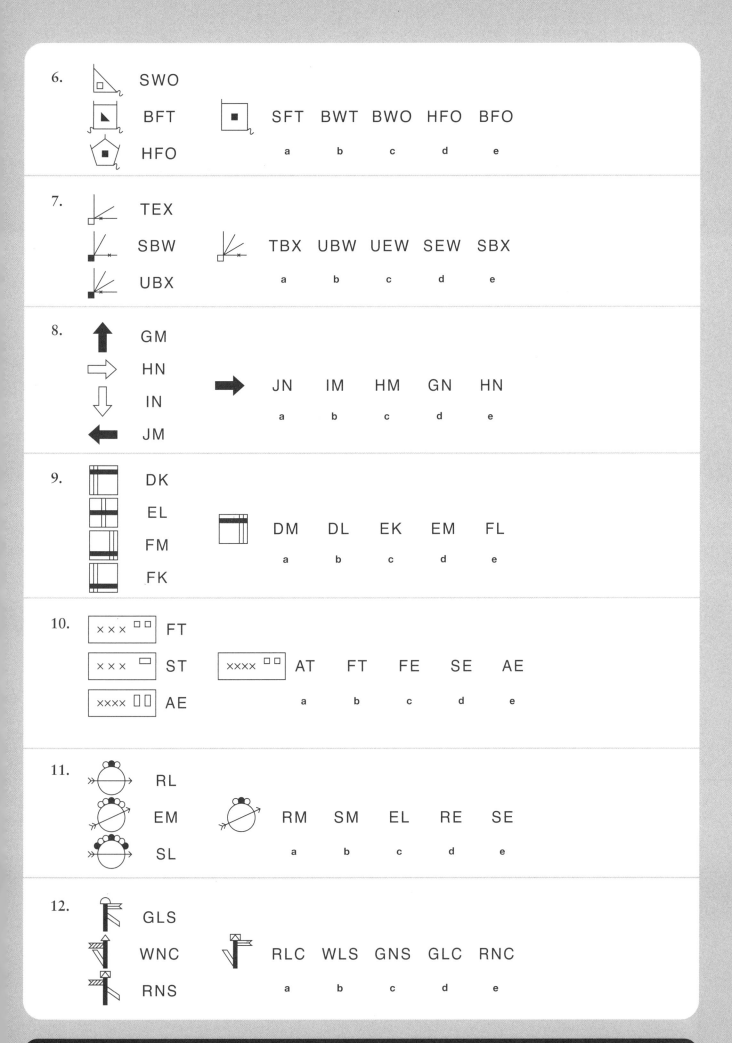

6.

SWO

BFT   SFT BWT BWO HFO BFO

HFO   a   b   c   d   e

7.

TEX

SBW   TBX UBW UEW SEW SBX

UBX   a   b   c   d   e

8.

GM

HN   JN   IM   HM   GN   HN

IN   a   b   c   d   e

JM

9.

DK

EL   DM   DL   EK   EM   FL

FM   a   b   c   d   e

FK

10.

FT

ST   AT   FT   FE   SE   AE

AE   a   b   c   d   e

11.

RL

EM   RM   SM   EL   RE   SE

SL   a   b   c   d   e

12.

GLS

WNC   RLC WLS GNS GLC RNC

RNS   a   b   c   d   e

TEST ADVICE

This information will not appear in the actual test.
It is included here to remind you not to stop working
until you are told the test is over.

CHECK YOUR ANSWERS AGAIN IF THERE IS TIME

FINDING ONE MISTAKE CAN MEAN EXTRA MARKS

Non-Verbal Reasoning
Multiple-Choice
Practice Test B

Read these instructions carefully:

1. You must not open or turn over this booklet until you are told to do so.

2. The booklet contains a multiple-choice test, in which you have to mark your answer to each question on the separate answer sheet.

3. There are five sections in this test. Each section starts with an explanation of what to do, followed by one or two examples with the answer marked on the answer sheet. You will then be asked to do some practice questions.

4. You should mark only one answer for each question.

5. Make sure that you draw a firm line clearly through the rectangle next to your answer. Rub out any mistakes as well as you can and put in your new answer.

6. Complete the questions as quickly and carefully as you can. If you find that you cannot do a question, do not waste time on it, go on to the next one.

7. You may do any rough working on a separate sheet of paper.

Section 1

In each of the questions below, there are two shapes on the left with an arrow between them. Look at them carefully and decide how the second shape is related to the first shape. There is then a third shape and another arrow followed by five more shapes. Decide which of the five shapes completes the second pair in the same way as the first pair. Mark it on your answer sheet.

Here is an example to help you.

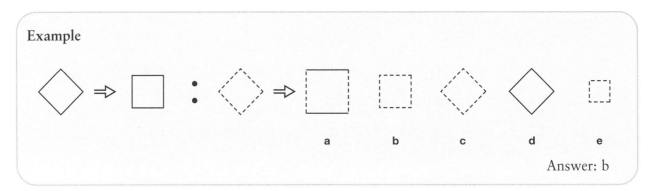

Example

a   b   c   d   e

Answer: b

Now try these practice questions.

P1.

a   b   c   d   e

P2.

a   b   c   d   e

WAIT UNTIL YOU ARE TOLD TO GO ON

1.

a   b   c   d   e

2.

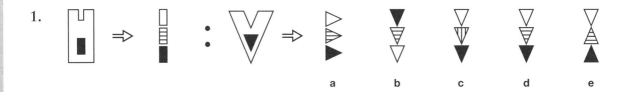

a   b   c   d   e

3.

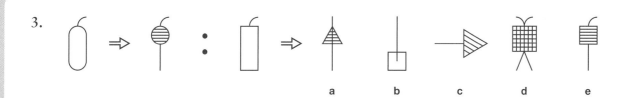

                                                   a   b   c   d   e

4.

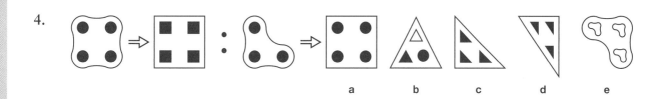

                                                 a   b   c   d   e

5.

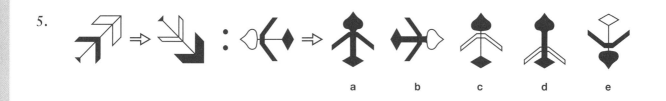

                                                 a   b   c   d   e

6.

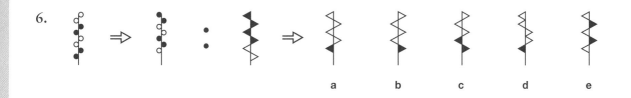

                                           a   b   c   d   e

7.

                                           a   b   c   d   e

8.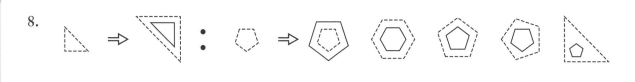

                                                a   b   c   d   e

9.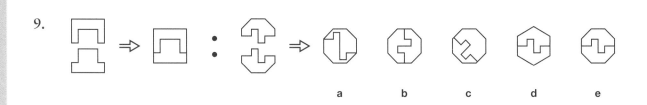

                                                a   b   c   d   e

10.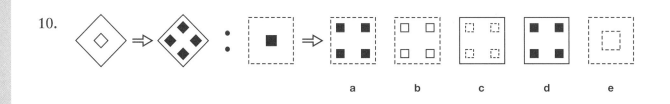

                                                a   b   c   d   e

11.

                                                a   b   c   d   e

12.

                                                a   b   c   d   e

Section 2

In the grids below, one square has been left empty. Look carefully at the five squares to the right and select the square that should complete the grid. Mark it on your answer sheet.

Here is an example to help you.

Example

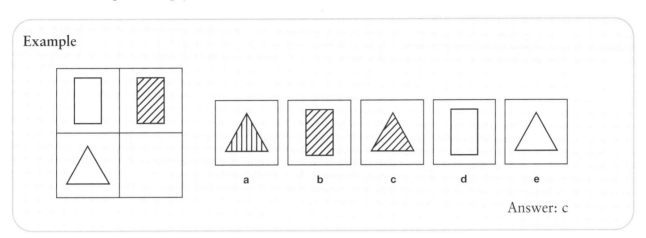

Answer: c

Now try these practice questions.

P1.

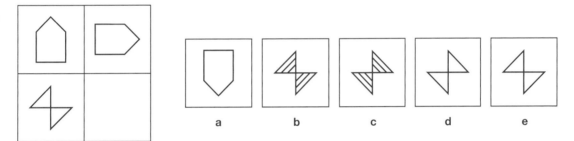

P2.

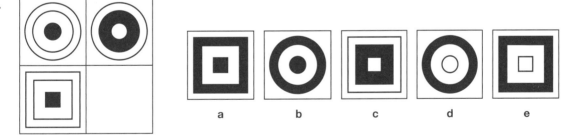

P3.

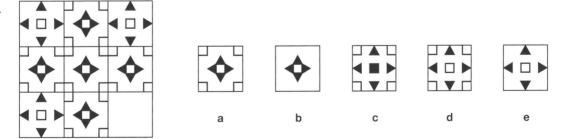

P4.

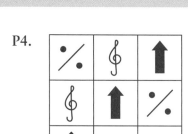
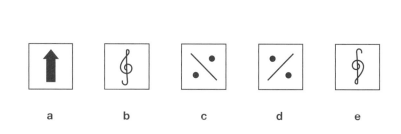

a   b   c   d   e

WAIT UNTIL YOU ARE TOLD TO GO ON

1.

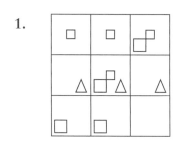 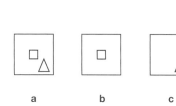 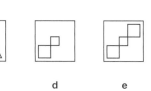

a   b   c   d   e

2.

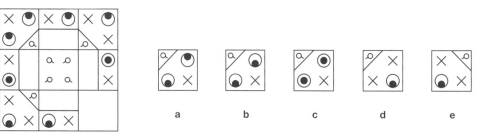

a   b   c   d   e

3.

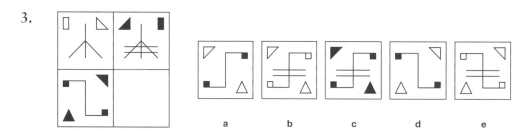

a   b   c   d   e

4.

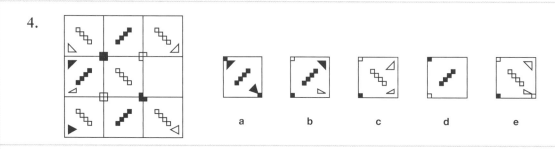

a   b   c   d   e

5.

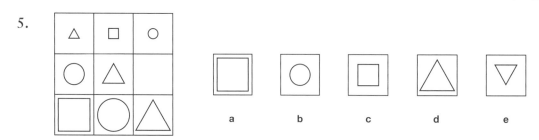

a   b   c   d   e

NOW GO ON TO THE NEXT PAGE

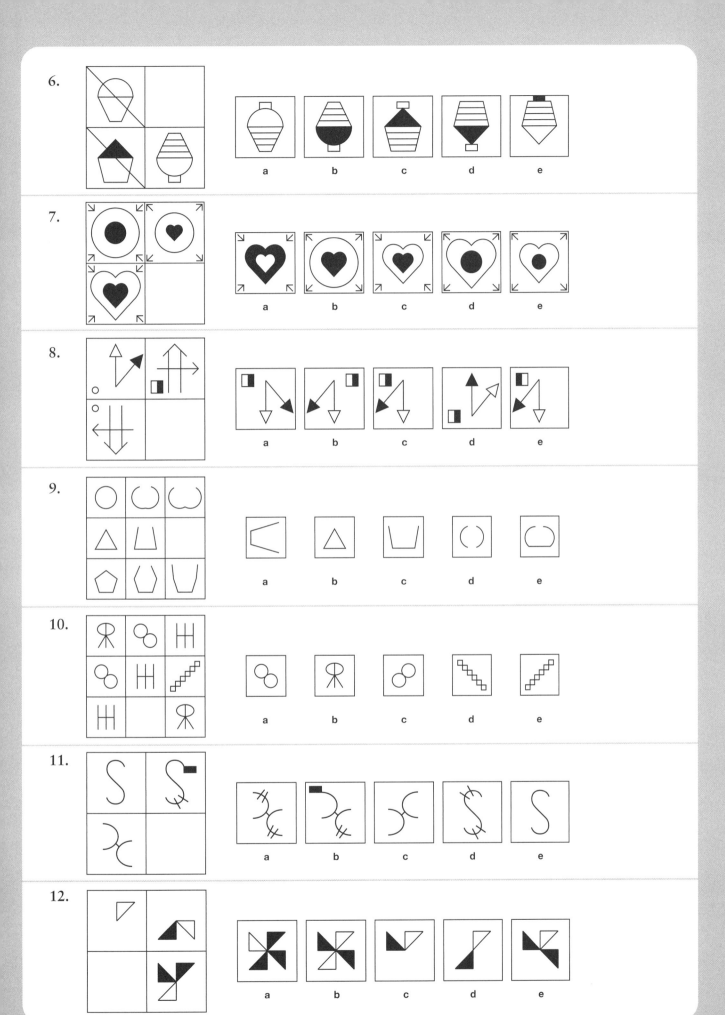

6.

7.

8.

9.

10.

11.

12.

In the questions below, you have to work out a code. You are given some shapes and the codes that go with them. Decide how the codes match the shapes. Then look at the test shape and find its correct code from the five given on the right. Mark it on your answer sheet.

Here are two examples to help you.

Look at Example 1.

Example 1

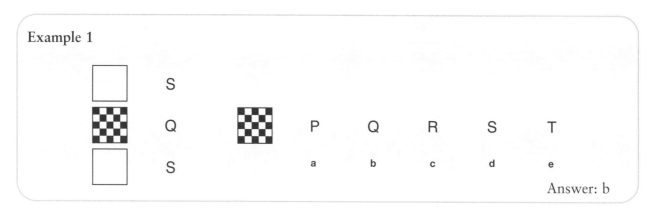

S stands for a white square and Q for a checked square, so the code for the test shape must be Q.

Now look at Example 2.

Example 2

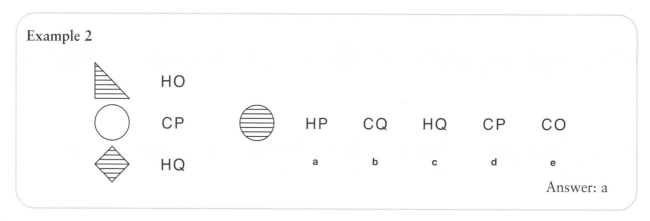

This time the shapes on the left have two letters. Find two shapes that have a letter in common. The first and the third shape both start with H, so H must be the code for shading. The second letter is different for each shape, so the second letter must be the code for shape. The test shape is a shaded circle, so its code is HP. HP is option *a*, so *a* is the correct answer.

Now try these practice questions.

P1.

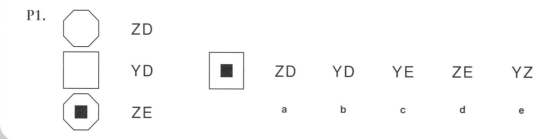

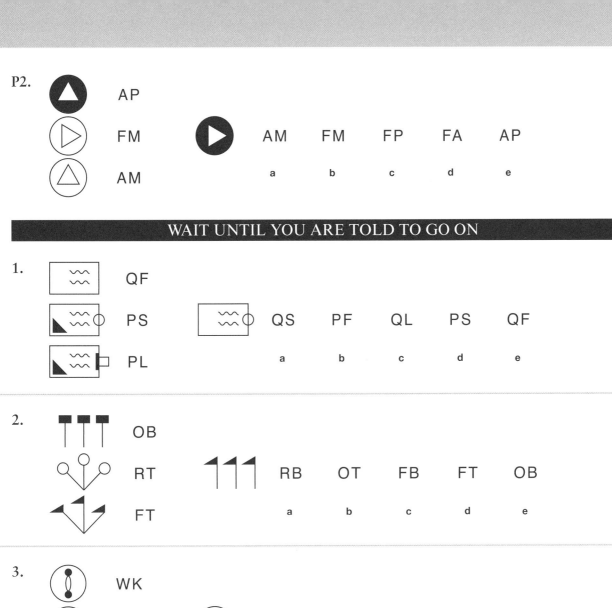

P2.

		a	b	c	d	e
● AP		AM	FM	FP	FA	AP
▷ FM	▶					
△ AM						

WAIT UNTIL YOU ARE TOLD TO GO ON

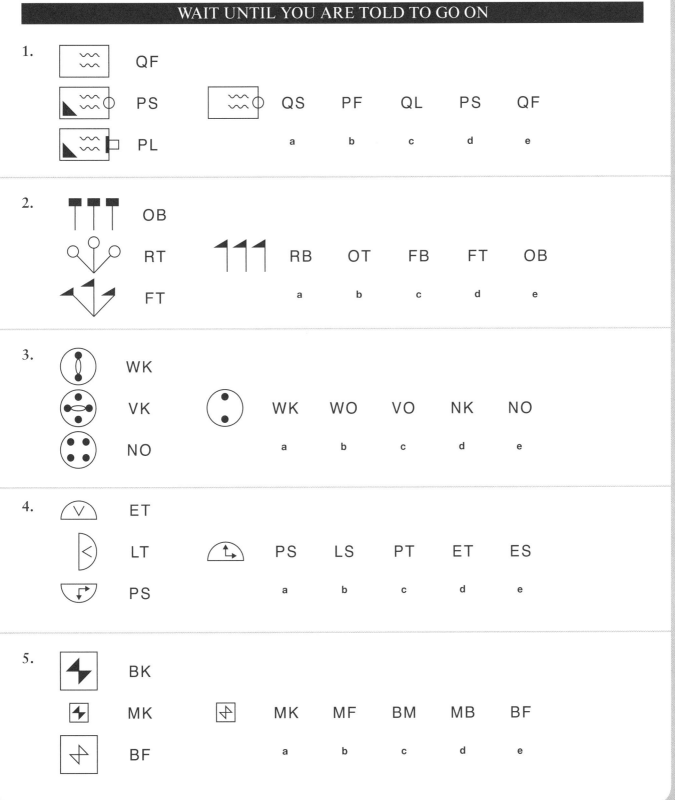

1.

		a	b	c	d	e
QF		QS	PF	QL	PS	QF
PS						
PL						

2.

		a	b	c	d	e
OB		RB	OT	FB	FT	OB
RT						
FT						

3.

		a	b	c	d	e
WK		WK	WO	VO	NK	NO
VK						
NO						

4.

		a	b	c	d	e
ET		PS	LS	PT	ET	ES
LT						
PS						

5.

		a	b	c	d	e
BK		MK	MF	BM	MB	BF
MK						
BF						

6. PF RS GT CS   GF GS RF CT CF
   a b c d e

7. ENP SAP RNT   EAT ENT RAT SAT SNT
   a b c d e

8. CD CT BD   BT BC TB CT DT
   a b c d e

9. US TS UL TJ   UJ TS LJ TL UL
   a b c d e

10. SPK SDJ TDK   TPJ TPK TDJ SPJ SDK
    a b c d e

11. FJL PJZ FWZ PRZ   PWL PJL FRL FRZ FJZ
    a b c d e

12. ZXU ZWV YXT   ZXT YWU YXV ZWT ZWU
    a b c d e

Section 4

In each of the questions below, there is a sequence of squares with one square left empty. Look at the five squares on the right and find the one that should take the place of the empty square to complete the sequence. Mark it on your answer sheet.

Here is an example to help you.

Example

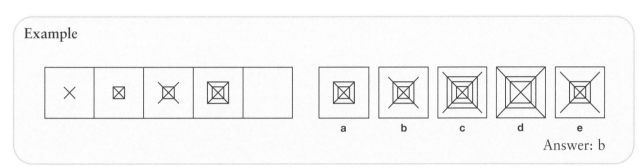

Answer: b

Now try these practice questions.

P1.

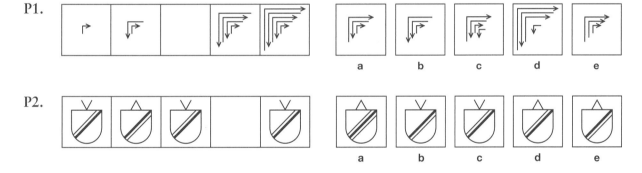

P2.

WAIT UNTIL YOU ARE TOLD TO GO ON

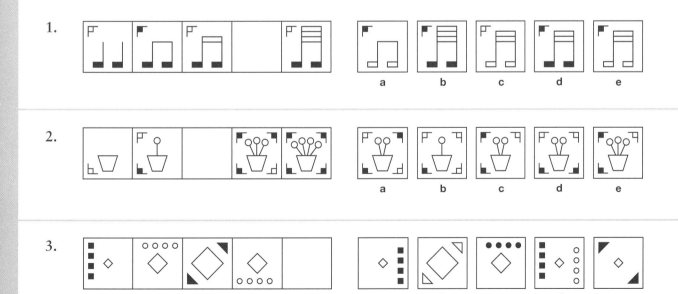

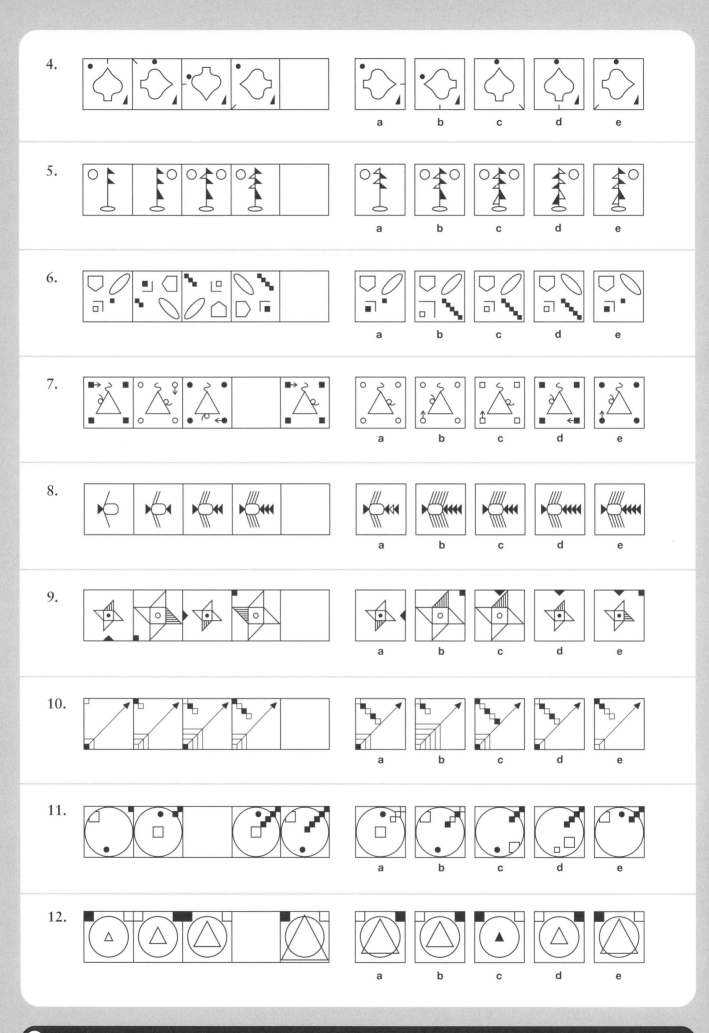

WAIT UNTIL YOU ARE TOLD TO GO ON

Section 5

In each question below, there are two shapes or patterns on the left which are similar in some way. Decide how they are similar. Find which of the five shapes on the right is most like the two shapes. Mark it on your answer sheet.

Here is an example to help you.

Example

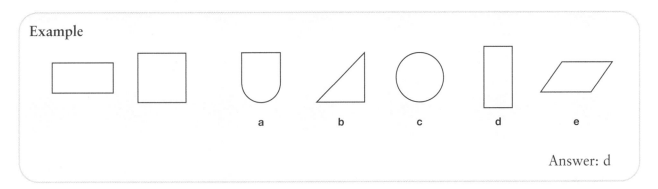

Answer: d

Now try these practice questions.

P1.

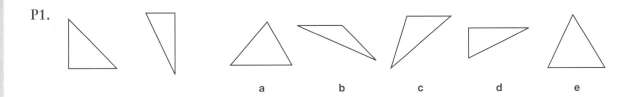

P2.

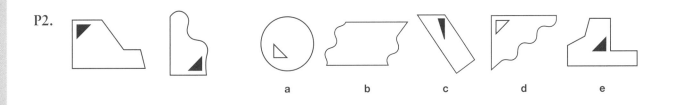

P3.

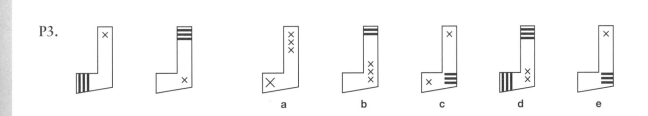

1.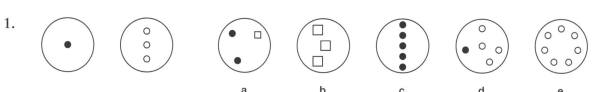

2.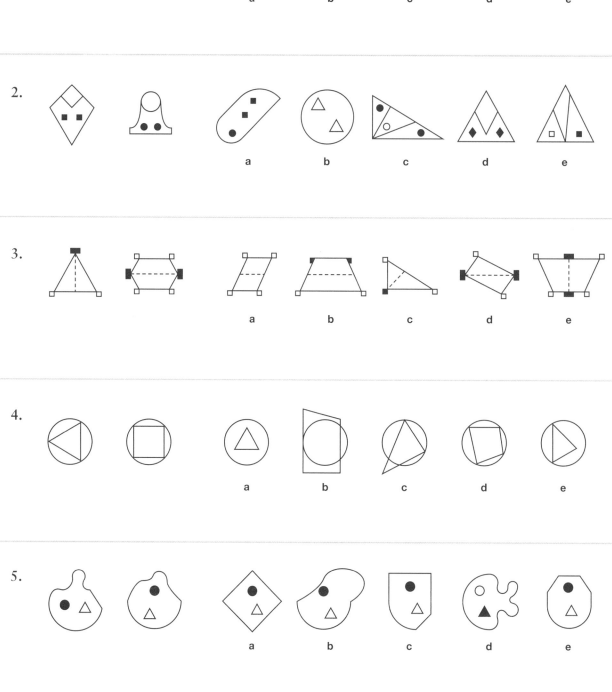

3.

4.

5.

6.

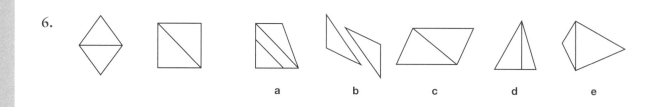

7.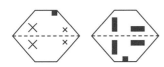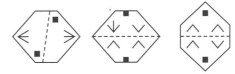

                                       a   b   c   d   e

8.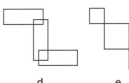

                                         a   b   c   d   e

9.

                                         a   b   c   d   e

10.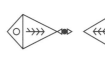

                                         a   b   c   d   e

11.   

                                         a   b   c   d   e

12.

                                         a   b   c   d   e

TEST ADVICE

This information will not appear in the actual test.
It is included here to remind you not to stop working
until you are told the test is over.

CHECK YOUR ANSWERS AGAIN IF THERE IS TIME

FINDING ONE MISTAKE CAN MEAN EXTRA MARKS

Non-Verbal Reasoning

Multiple-Choice
Practice Test C

Read these instructions carefully:

1. You must not open or turn over this booklet until you are told to do so.

2. The booklet contains a multiple-choice test, in which you have to mark your answer to each question on the separate answer sheet.

3. There are five sections in this test. Each section starts with an explanation of what to do, followed by one or two examples with the answer marked on the answer sheet. You will then be asked to do some practice questions.

4. You should mark only one answer for each question.

5. Make sure that you draw a firm line clearly through the rectangle next to your answer. Rub out any mistakes as well as you can and put in your new answer.

6. Complete the questions as quickly and carefully as you can. If you find that you cannot do a question, do not waste time on it, go on to the next one.

7. You may do any rough working on a separate sheet of paper.

Section 1

In each of the questions below, there is a sequence of squares with one square left empty. Look at the five squares on the right and find the one that should take the place of the empty square to complete the sequence. Mark it on your answer sheet.

Here is an example to help you.

Example

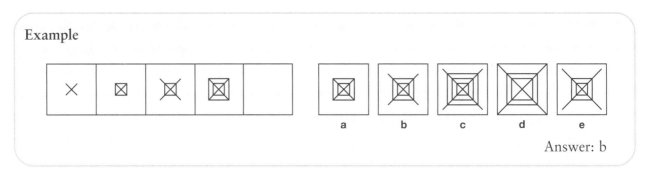

Answer: b

Now try these practice questions.

P1.

P2.

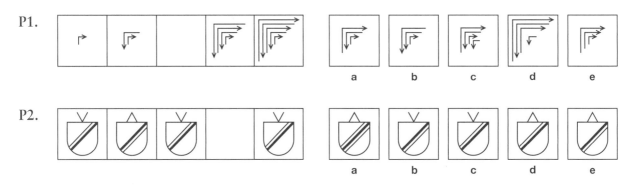

WAIT UNTIL YOU ARE TOLD TO GO ON

1.

2.

3.

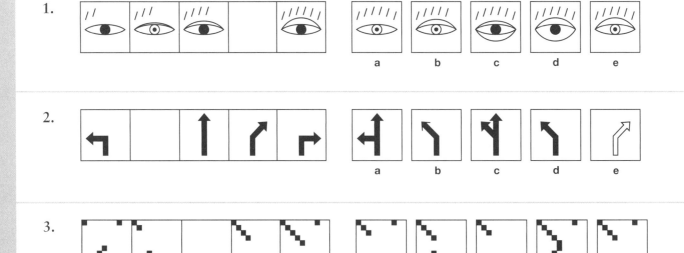

NOW GO ON TO THE NEXT PAGE

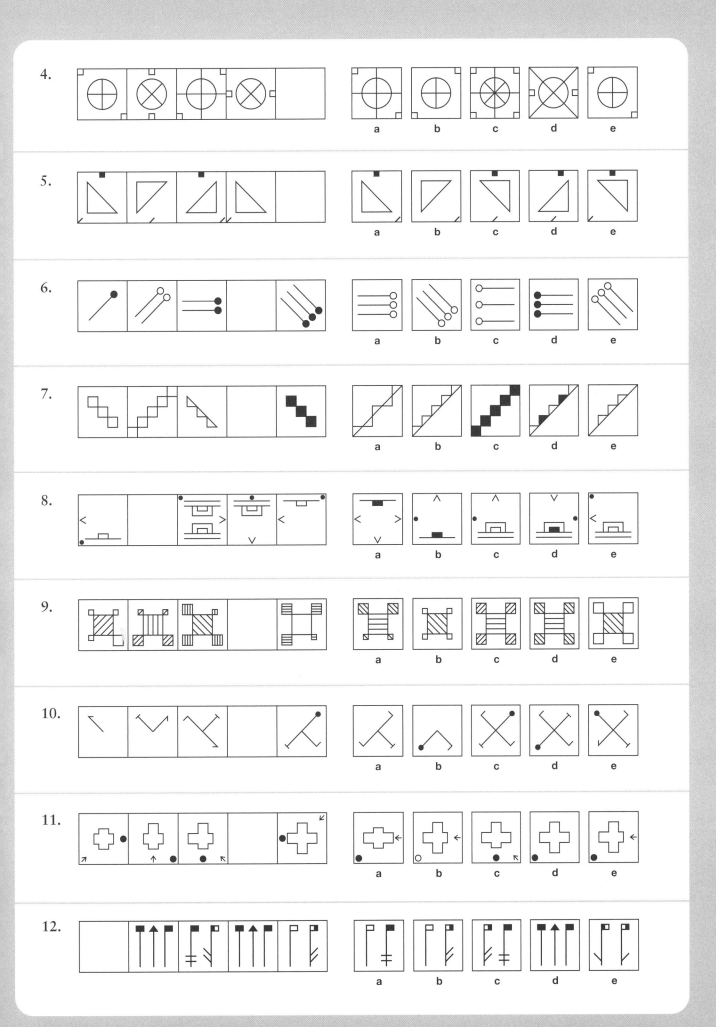

Section 2

In the grids below, one square has been left empty. Look carefully at the five squares to the right and select the square that should complete the grid. Mark it on your answer sheet.

Here is an example to help you.

Example

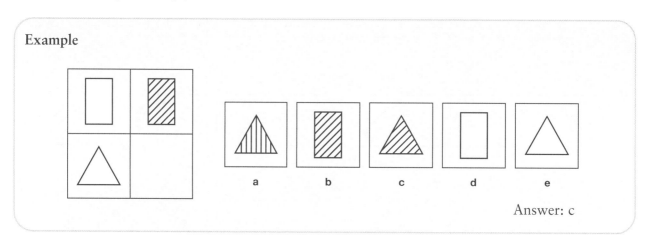

Answer: c

Now try these practice questions.

P1.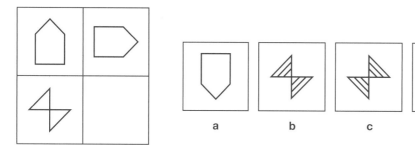

P2.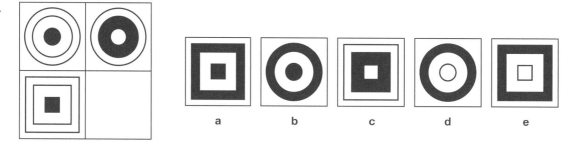

P3.

NOW GO ON TO THE NEXT PAGE

P4.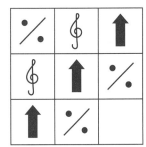

                              a   b   c   d   e

WAIT UNTIL YOU ARE TOLD TO GO ON

1.

                              a   b   c   d   e

2.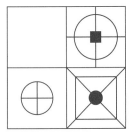

                              a   b   c   d   e

3.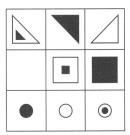

                              a   b   c   d   e

4.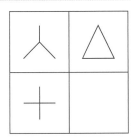

                              a   b   c   d   e

5.

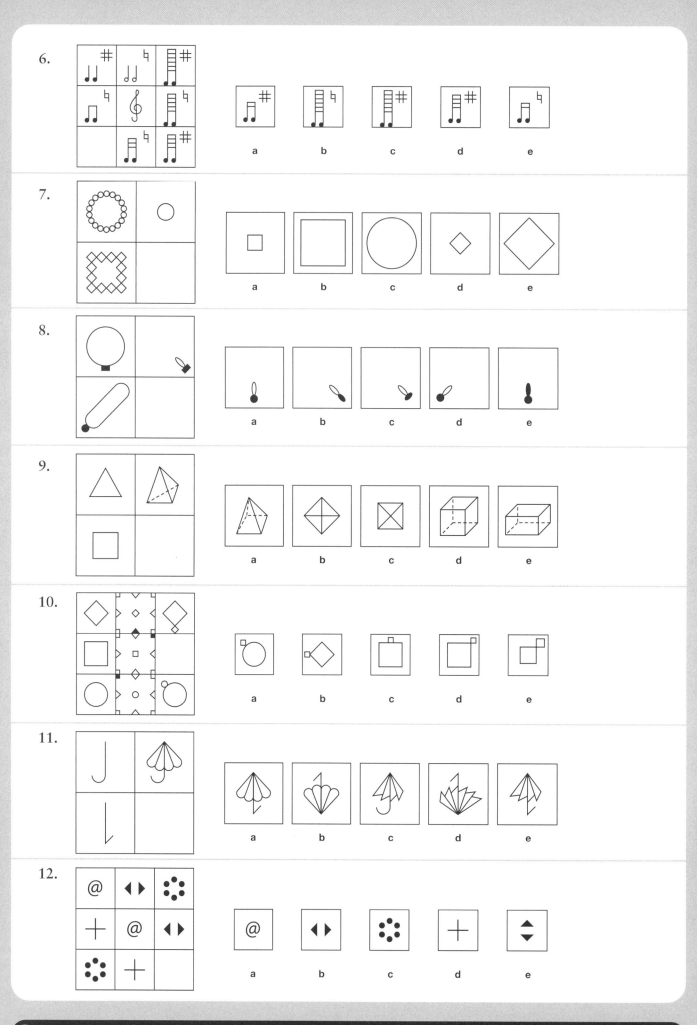

WAIT UNTIL YOU ARE TOLD TO GO ON

Section 3

In each of the questions below, there are two shapes on the left with an arrow between them. Look at them carefully and decide how the second shape is related to the first shape. There is then a third shape and another arrow followed by five more shapes. Decide which of the five shapes completes the second pair in the same way as the first pair. Mark it on your answer sheet.

Here is an example to help you.

Example

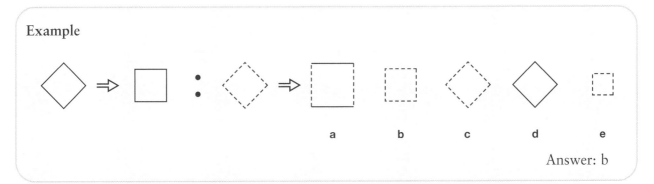

a   b   c   d   e

Answer: b

Now try these practice questions.

P1.

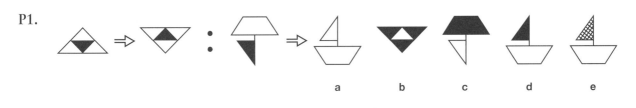

a   b   c   d   e

P2.

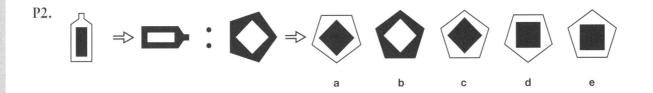

a   b   c   d   e

WAIT UNTIL YOU ARE TOLD TO GO ON

1.

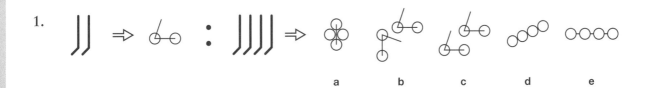

a   b   c   d   e

2.

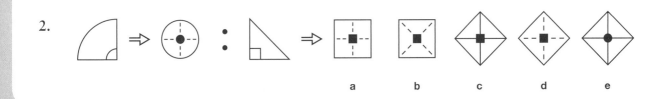

a   b   c   d   e

3.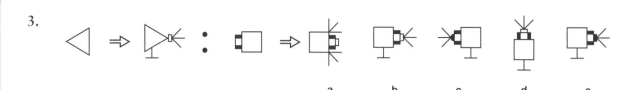

a   b   c   d   e

4.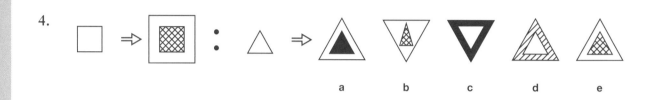

a   b   c   d   e

5.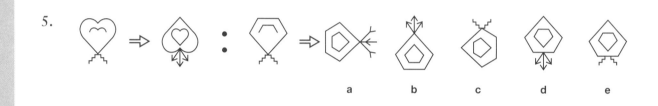

a   b   c   d   e

6.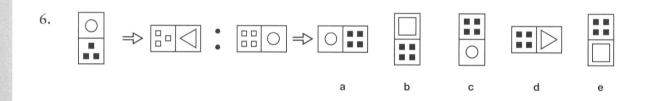

a   b   c   d   e

7.

a   b   c   d   e

8.

                                            a   b   c   d   e

9.

                                      a   b   c   d   e

10.

                                      a   b   c   d   e

11.

                                      a   b   c   d   e

12.

                                      a   b   c   d   e

In the questions below, you have to work out a code. You are given some shapes and the codes that go with them. Decide how the codes match the shapes. Then look at the test shape and find its correct code from the five given on the right. Mark it on your answer sheet.

Here are two examples to help you.

Look at Example 1.

Example 1

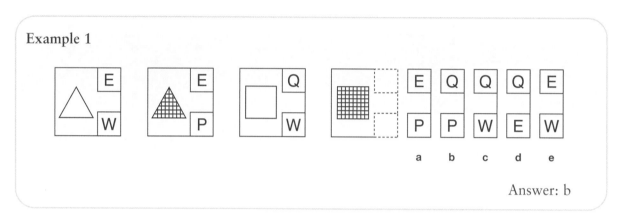

Answer: b

The top letter is for the shape, with E for triangle and Q for square.
The lower letter is for the type of shading, W is for white and P for checked.
So the code for the checked square is QP, which is option *b*.

Now look at Example 2.

Example 2

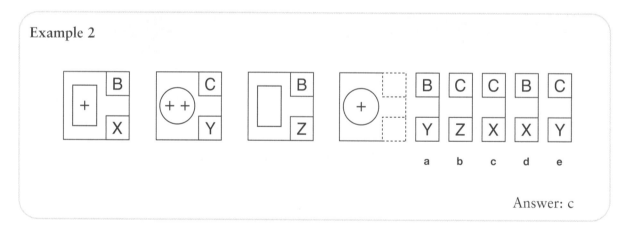

Answer: c

In this example, the top letter again refers to the shape. A rectangle is code B and a circle is code C. In each of the three shapes given, there is a different code for the second letter, so this letter must be linked with the pattern inside the shape. One cross is code X, so the given pattern is code CX. CX is option *c*, so *c* is the answer.

Now try these practice questions.

P1.

P2.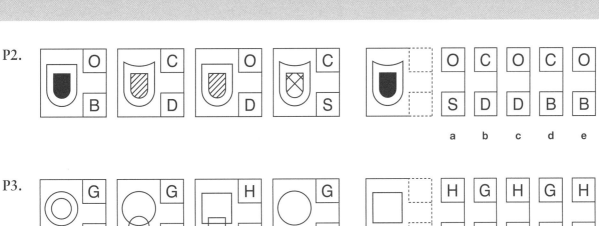

	a	b	c	d	e
	O	C	O	C	O
	S	D	D	B	B

P3.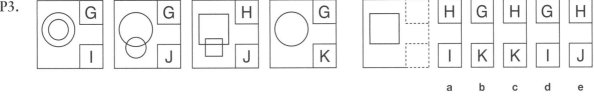

	a	b	c	d	e
	H	G	H	G	H
	I	K	K	I	J

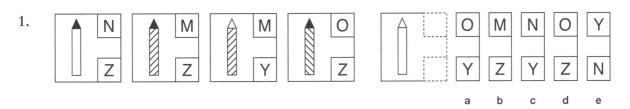

WAIT UNTIL YOU ARE TOLD TO GO ON

1.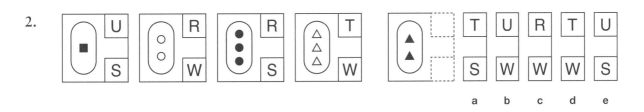

	a	b	c	d	e
	O	M	N	O	Y
	Y	Z	Y	Z	N

2.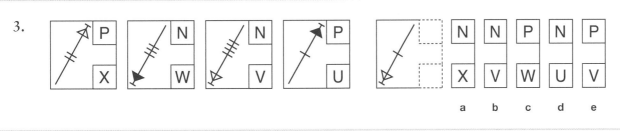

	a	b	c	d	e
	T	U	R	T	U
	S	W	W	W	S

3.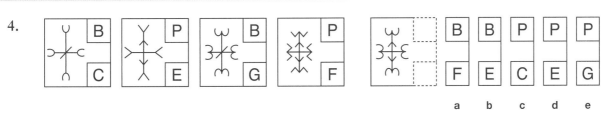

	a	b	c	d	e
	N	N	P	N	P
	X	V	W	U	V

4.

	a	b	c	d	e
	B	B	P	P	P
	F	E	C	E	G

5.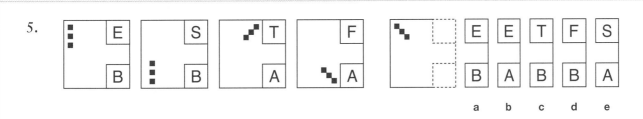

	a	b	c	d	e
	E	E	T	F	S
	B	A	B	B	A

6.

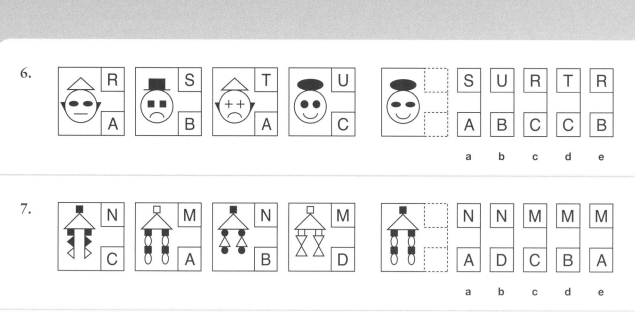

S	U	R	T	R
A	B	C	C	B
a	b	c	d	e

7.

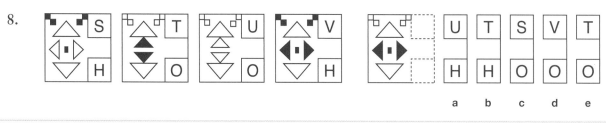

N	N	M	M	M
A	D	C	B	A
a	b	c	d	e

8.

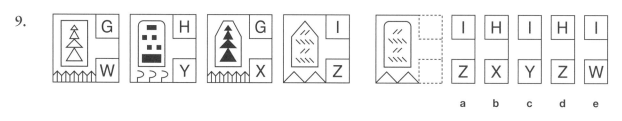

U	T	S	V	T
H	H	O	O	O
a	b	c	d	e

9.

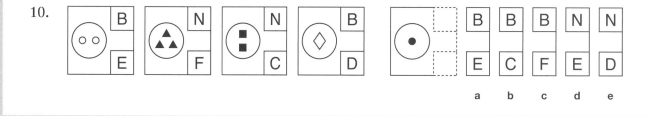

I	H	I	H	I
Z	X	Y	Z	W
a	b	c	d	e

10.

B	B	B	N	N
E	C	F	E	D
a	b	c	d	e

11.

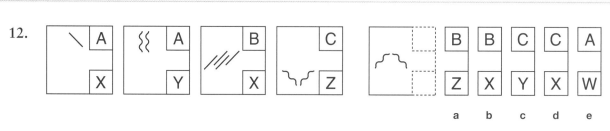

K	L	J	I	L
N	O	M	O	M
a	b	c	d	e

12.

B	B	C	C	A
Z	X	Y	X	W
a	b	c	d	e

The following questions are about finding the odd one out in a series of shapes or patterns. Find the odd one out and mark it on your answer sheet.

Here is an example to help you.

Example

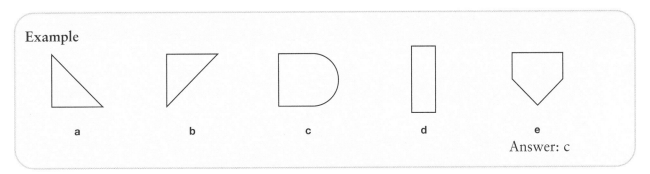

Answer: c

Look carefully at the five shapes. They have differing numbers of sides, but all are made of straight sides except for shape *c*, so *c* is the odd one out.

Now try these practice questions.

P1.

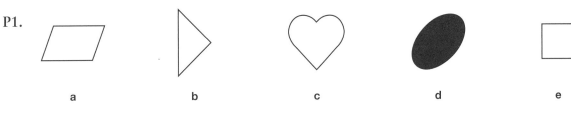

P2.

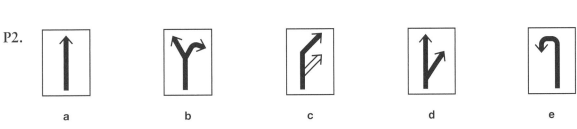

WAIT UNTIL YOU ARE TOLD TO GO ON

1.

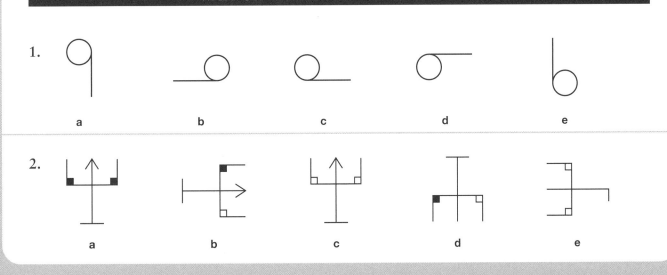

2.

NOW GO ON TO THE NEXT PAGE

3.

a

b

c

d

e

4.

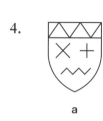
a

b

c

d

e

5.

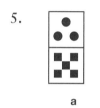
a

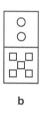
b

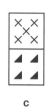
c

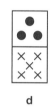
d

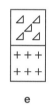
e

6.

a

b

c

d

e

7.

a

b

c

d

e

8.

a   b   c   d   e

9.

a   b   c   d   e

10.

a   b   c   d   e

11.

a   b   c   d   e

12.

a   b   c   d   e

TEST ADVICE

This information will not appear in the actual test.
It is included here to remind you not to stop working
until you are told the test is over.

CHECK YOUR ANSWERS AGAIN IF THERE IS TIME

FINDING ONE MISTAKE CAN MEAN EXTRA MARKS

Non-Verbal Reasoning
Multiple-Choice
Practice Test D

Read these instructions carefully:

1. You must not open or turn over this booklet until you are told to do so.

2. The booklet contains a multiple-choice test, in which you have to mark your answer to each question on the separate answer sheet.

3. There are five sections in this test. Each section starts with an explanation of what to do, followed by one or two examples with the answer marked on the answer sheet. You will then be asked to do some practice questions.

4. You should mark only one answer for each question.

5. Make sure that you draw a firm line clearly through the rectangle next to your answer. Rub out any mistakes as well as you can and put in your new answer.

6. Complete the questions as quickly and carefully as you can. If you find that you cannot do a question, do not waste time on it, go on to the next one.

7. You may do any rough working on a separate sheet of paper.

Section 1

In the grids below, one square has been left empty. Look carefully at the five squares to the right and select the square that should complete the grid. Mark it on your answer sheet.

Here is an example to help you.

Example

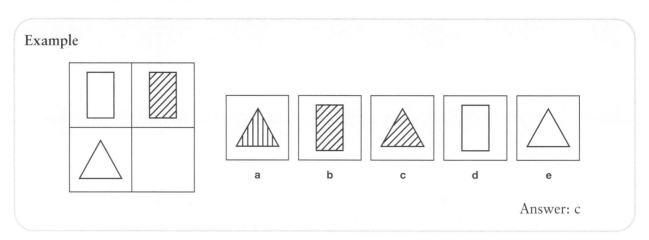

Answer: c

Now try these practice questions.

P1.

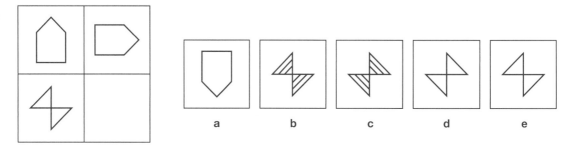

P2.

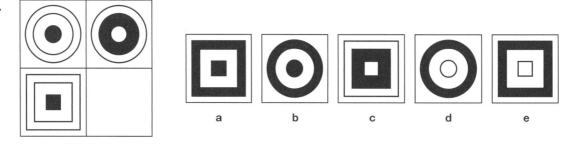

P3.

a   b   c   d   e

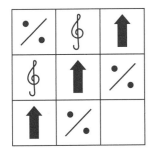

          a   b   c   d   e

WAIT UNTIL YOU ARE TOLD TO GO ON

1.

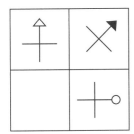

          a   b   c   d   e

2.

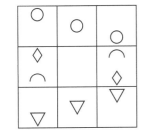

          a   b   c   d   e

3.

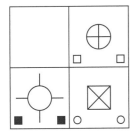

          a   b   c   d   e

4.

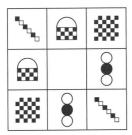

          a   b   c   d   e

5.

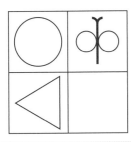

          a   b   c   d   e

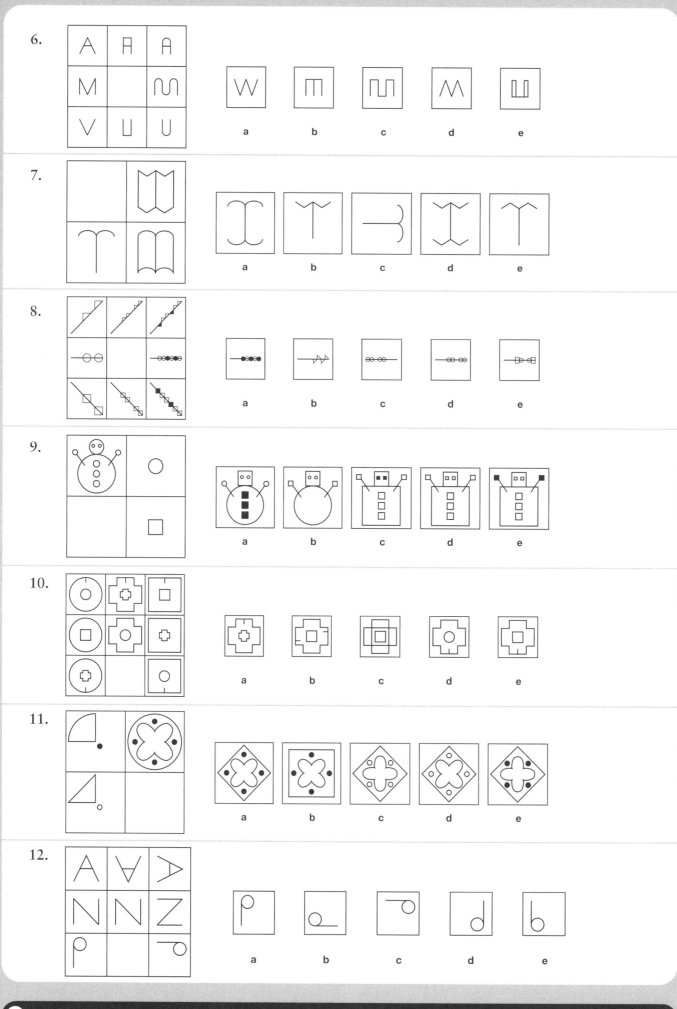

Section 2

In each of the questions below, there are two shapes on the left with an arrow between them. Look at them carefully and decide how the second shape is related to the first shape. There is then a third shape and another arrow followed by five more shapes. Decide which of the five shapes completes the second pair in the same way as the first pair. Mark it on your answer sheet.

Here is an example to help you.

Example

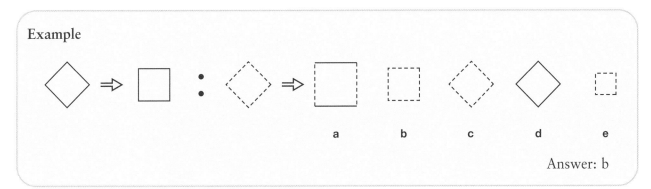

a   b   c   d   e

Answer: b

Now try these practice questions.

P1.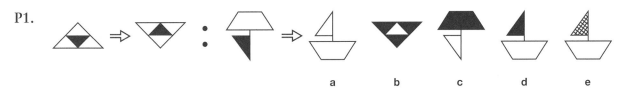

a   b   c   d   e

P2.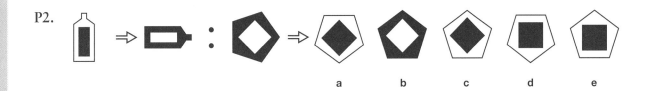

a   b   c   d   e

WAIT UNTIL YOU ARE TOLD TO GO ON

1.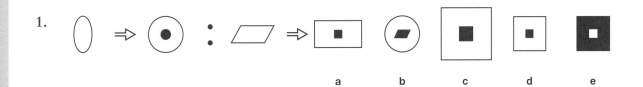

a   b   c   d   e

2.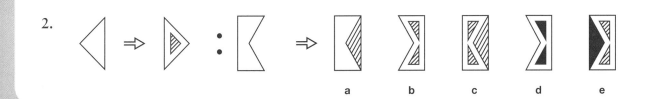

a   b   c   d   e

NOW GO ON TO THE NEXT PAGE

3.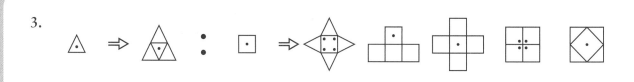

a   b   c   d   e

4.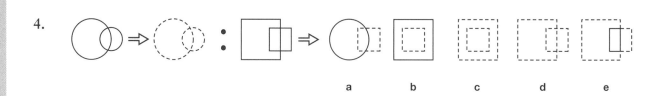

a   b   c   d   e

5.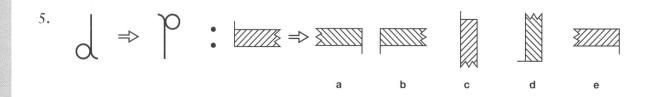

a   b   c   d   e

6.

a   b   c   d   e

7.

a   b   c   d   e

8.

        a   b   c   d   e

9.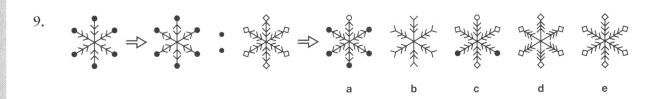

        a   b   c   d   e

10.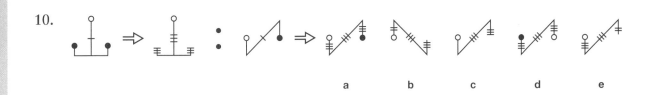

        a   b   c   d   e

11.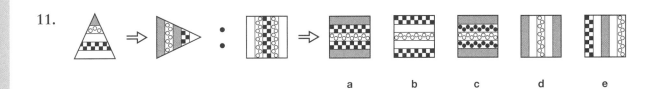

        a   b   c   d   e

12.

        a   b   c   d   e

Section 3

In each of the questions below, there is a sequence of squares with one square left empty. Look at the five squares on the right and find the one that should take the place of the empty square to complete the sequence. Mark it on your answer sheet.

Here is an example to help you.

Example

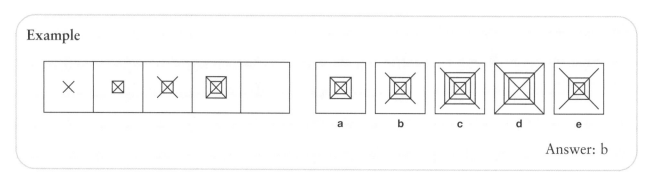

Answer: b

Now try these practice questions.

P1.

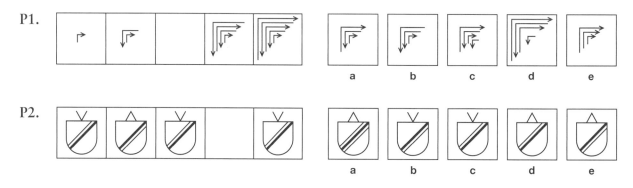

P2.

WAIT UNTIL YOU ARE TOLD TO GO ON

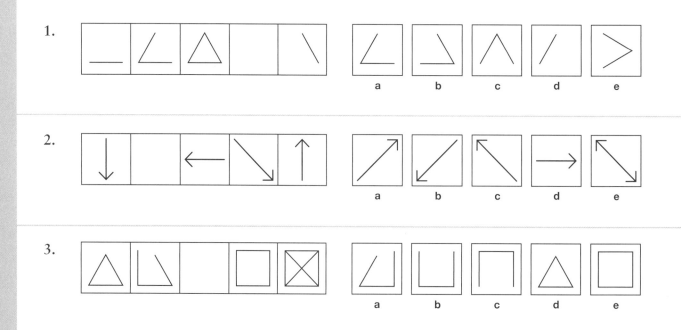

1.

2.

3.

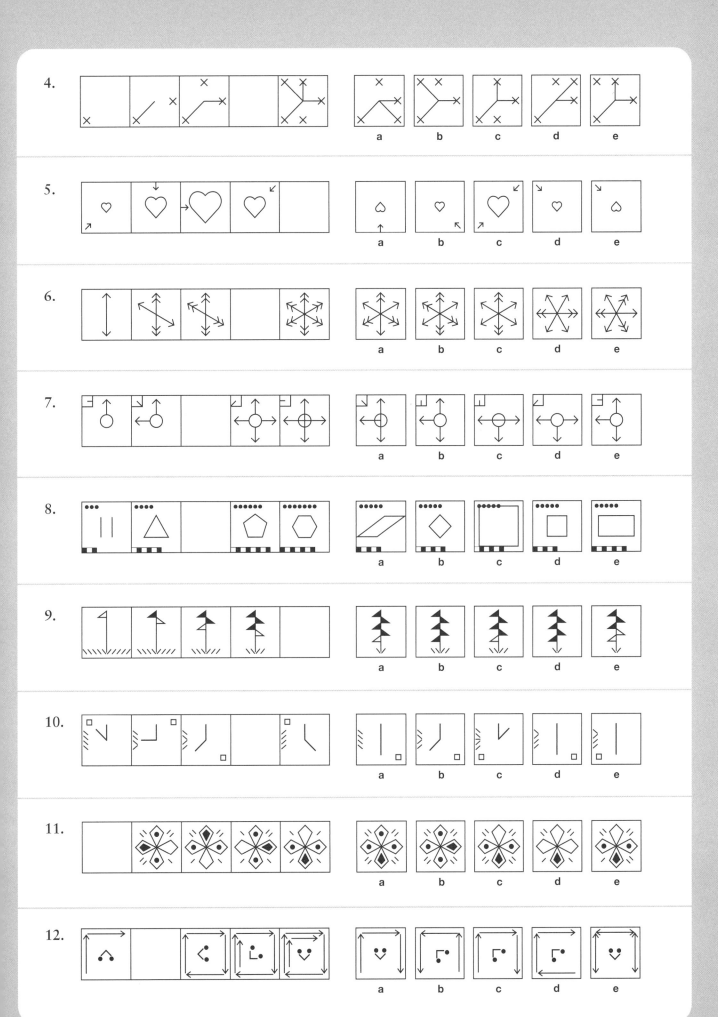

Section 4

The following questions are about finding the odd one out in a series of shapes or patterns. Find the odd one out and mark it on the answer sheet.

Here is an example to help you.

Example

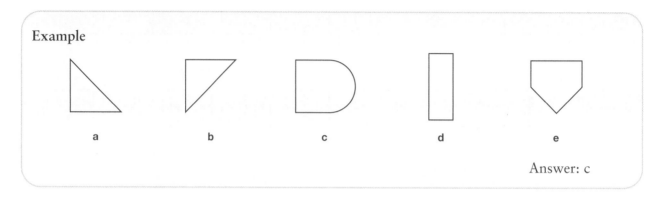

| | a | | b | | c | | d | | e | |

Answer: c

Look carefully at the five shapes. They have differing numbers of sides, but all are made of straight sides except for shape *c*, so *c* is the odd one out.

Now try these practice questions.

P1.

    a   b   c   d   e

P2.

    a   b   c   d   e

WAIT UNTIL YOU ARE TOLD TO GO ON

1.

    a   b   c   d   e

2.

    a   b   c   d   e

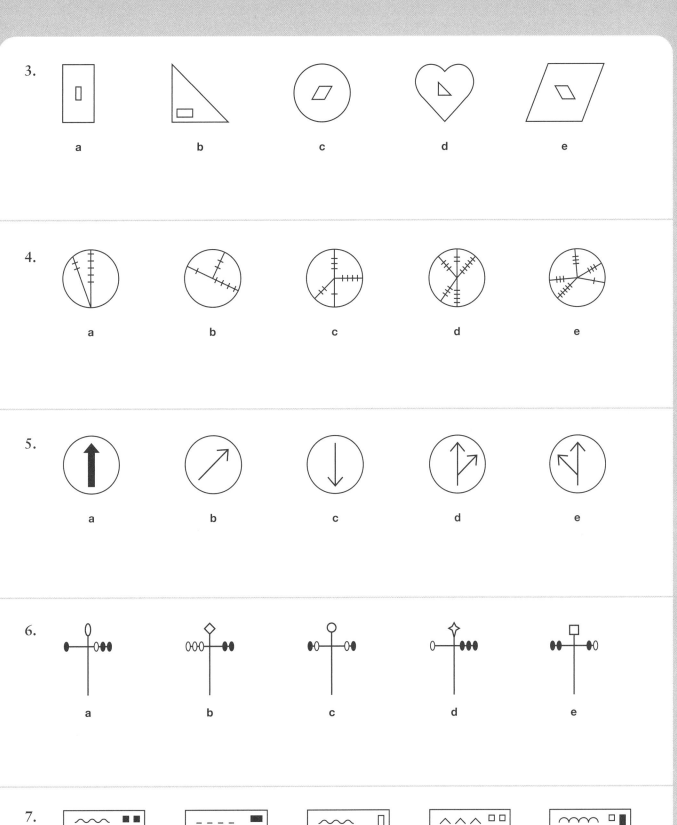

3.

    a   b   c   d   e

4.

    a   b   c   d   e

5.

    a   b   c   d   e

6.

    a   b   c   d   e

7.

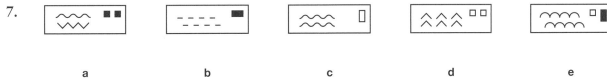

    a   b   c   d   e

8.

a   b   c   d   e

9.

a   b   c   d   e

10.

a   b   c   d   e

11.

a   b   c   d   e

12.

a   b   c   d   e

In the questions below, you have to work out a code. You are given some shapes and the codes that go with them. Decide how the codes match the shapes. Then look at the test shape and find its correct code from the five given on the right. Mark it on your answer sheet.

Here are two examples to help you.

Look at Example 1.

Example 1

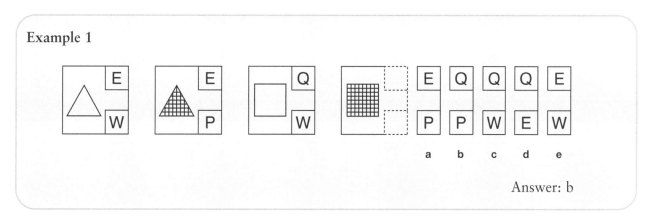

Answer: b

The top letter is for the shape, with E for triangle and Q for square.
The lower letter is for the type of shading, W is for white and P for checked.
So the code for the checked square is QP, which is option *b*.

Now look at Example 2.

Example 2

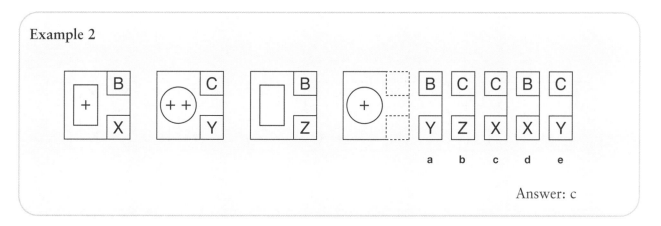

Answer: c

In this example, the top letter again refers to the shape. A rectangle is code B and a circle is code C. In each of the three shapes given, there is a different code for the second letter, so this letter must be linked with the pattern inside the shape. One cross is code X, so the given pattern is code CX. CX is option *c*, so *c* is the answer.

Now try these practice questions.

P1.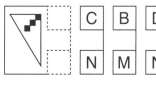

P2.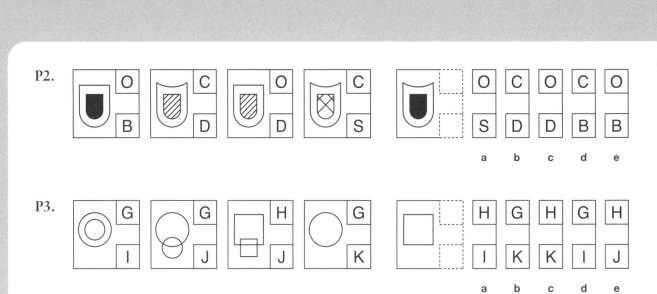

P3.

WAIT UNTIL YOU ARE TOLD TO GO ON

1.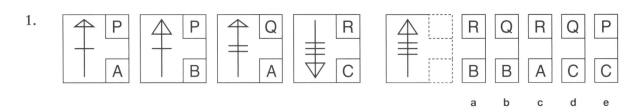

2.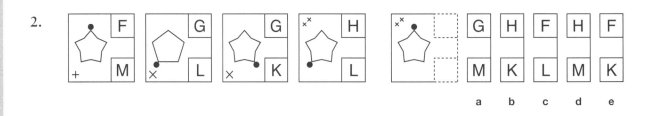

3.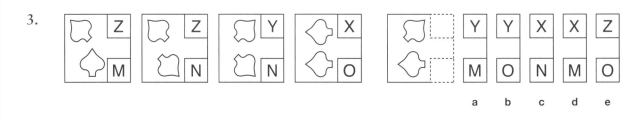

4.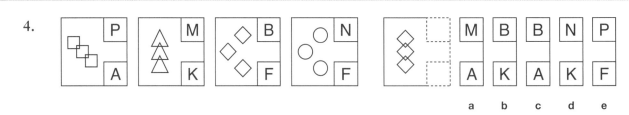

5.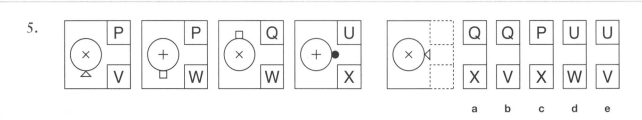

6.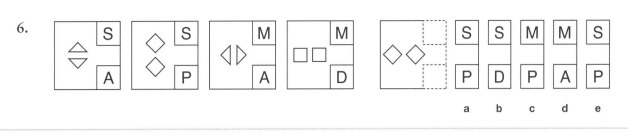

a   b   c   d   e

7.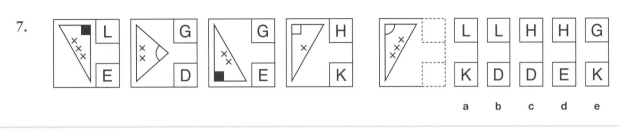

a   b   c   d   e

8.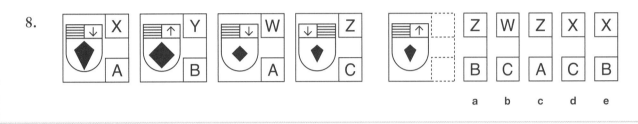

a   b   c   d   e

9.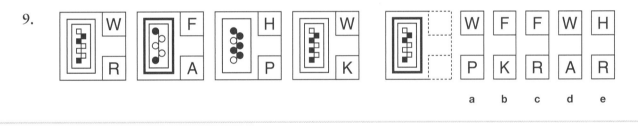

a   b   c   d   e

10.

a   b   c   d   e

11.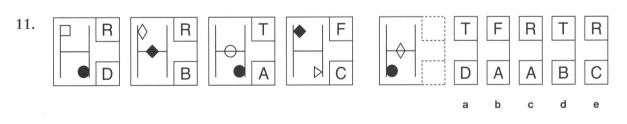

a   b   c   d   e

12.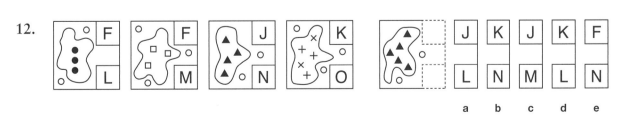

a   b   c   d   e

TEST ADVICE

This information will not appear in the actual test.
It is included here to remind you not to stop working
until you are told the test is over.

CHECK YOUR ANSWERS AGAIN IF THERE IS TIME

FINDING ONE MISTAKE CAN MEAN EXTRA MARKS

Letts

PRACTICE PAPERS

Answers and Explanations

Non-verbal Reasoning

Marking

Allow one mark for each correct answer. Half marks are not allowed, and marks are not given for 'very nearly correct answers'! No marks are deducted for wrong answers.

If scores are low, look at the paper and identify which question types seem to be harder for your child. Then spend some time going over them together. If your child is very accurate and gets correct answers, but works too slowly, try doing one of the practice papers with time targets going through. By being helpful and looking for ways to help your child, they will grow in confidence and feel well prepared when they take the actual examinations.

Practice Test A Answers and Explanations

Section 1

Eg. b
Square is placed around the X, then in the next box the X extends, then another square is placed around the extended X, and so on.

P1. a
New arrow added each time, going in the opposite direction to the previously added arrow.

P2. e
Top V inverts each time, and the line that is bold alternates in each box.

1. d
Crosses in top left corner increase by 1, and crosses in bottom right corner decrease by 1. There is always + in bottom left corner, and there is one X in centre.

2. c
Dots in top left corner and bottom right corner increase by 1, and the shape in the middle turns clockwise.

3. b
Middle square remains solid shaded, and small squares across top right and bottom left corner increase by 2 each time.

4. a
Horizontal lines increase by 1, and the bottom corner squares decrease by 1. Note that the vertical central pole always has a flat top.

5. b
Alternate shapes, turning clockwise 45°.

6. d
Alternate shapes are hearts with short lines at north, east, south and west.

7. a
Alternate shapes have a solid stalk, the short lines increase by 2 each time, and the centre spot enlarges.

8. a
Triangles and lines are removed gradually each time.

9. b
In alternate boxes, the small dot moves to the diagonal opposite corner and the shape in the centre turns anticlockwise 45°.

10. b
Dots in centre increase by 1 each time, and the external dot moves clockwise round vertices.

11. d
Pattern applies to every other box, prongs increase by 1 each side, with the shape turning clockwise 45° each time, and alternate sections have broad base for prongs.

12. e
Reflecting pattern to give the arrows pointing to centre from top left and bottom right corners, and white triangle at bottom left.

Section 2

Eg. d
Quadrilateral with only right angles.

P1. d
Right-angled triangles.

P2. e
Small dark right-angled triangle inside each shape.

P3. e
One small x inside each shape.

1. d
3 intersecting triangles including 2 right-angled, and 2 meeting at a vertex.

2. e
2 intersecting squares, 2 right-angled triangles, and 1 spade all arranged around the edge of the square.

3. a
Square with 4 congruent clear shapes inside, all pointing in the same direction.

4. b
2 clear circles as wheels, and 1 dark square inside.

5. c
Circle with 2 equal dark shapes, and 2 clear shapes on the circumference.

6. c
+ inside, clear shape inside, and circle with dark dot on perimeter.

7. e
3 clear squares, and 2 small dark squares as extensions inside the extended sides of a large square.

8. d
3 vertical lines inside the shape.

9. e
Lozenge with two rounded ends.

10. d
Dotted outline with a cross at the top.

11. d
2 clear and 1 dark triangle inside, all touching the dotted interior sides. Note that the dotted border is different in option a.

12. d
3 wiggly lines on each side of the shape.

Section 3

Eg. b

Same shape, rotated 45°.

P1. d

Shape is inverted.

P2. a

Shape is turned with the shading reversed.

1. c

Shape is rotated 180°.

2. d

Same shapes connected at the tip, horizontal lines on the left, and vertical lines on the right.

3. d

Bold outline, top line moves to the bottom, *moved to diagonally opposite corner.

4. e

1 large clear square, and 2 small dark squares pointing in same direction.

5. e

Top left and bottom right shapes combined and moved to top left, and the others move to the bottom right.

6. d

3 smaller congruent shapes – dark, striped and clear.

7. d

Dots become squares, the position is reversed, and it is solid at the top and clear at the bottom.

8. b

Large dark shapes move to the opposite side and become light, and small light shapes move to the opposite side and become dark. Orientation of the large shapes remains the same.

9. b

First square becomes $\frac{1}{4}$ of the larger square, top left shape moves to the middle corners, bottom right shape moves to the bottom left and bottom right corners.

10. c

External straight lines become curved.

11. b

Shape rotates 90° anticlockwise, and the semicircle has horizontal stripes.

12. e

Reflected with the vertical lines becoming horizontal lines.

Section 4

Eg. c

Right shape is the same as the left but has diagonal lines inside.

P1. d

Right shape is left shape turned 90°.

P2. c

Right shape is the same as the left, but the inner layer goes from dark to light and the middle layer goes from light to dark.

P3. e

Each corner box has the same pattern.

P4. b

Each row and each column has one of the 3 shapes.

1. b

Diagonal opposite corners are the same.

2. d

Left boxes in top and bottom rows reflect in the right boxes.

3. d

Shapes going from right to left turn 90° anticlockwise.

4. b

Shapes are enlarged going from left to right, and bottom shape gains horizontal lines.

5. a

Bottom boxes are a reflection of the top boxes, with one extra X and shape.

6. b

Each row has its own shape, getting larger moving right. Each row and each column has a clear, dark and cross-hatched shape.

7. c

Boxes on the right are the same as the left, but there is a circle in the bottom right linked to the central shape, with different shading to the central shape which is now a square. The top right triangle also changes shading.

8. b

In the middle row there are light circles in the right corners, and dark squares in the bottom left corner.

9. a

Shape stays the same going to the right box, except the 2 dark triangles become light.

10. e

Going to the right box, the shapes are inverted and the colours are reversed.

11. e

Dots increase by 1 in each box, whilst the window shape moves lower.

12. c

Same shapes in each row, and each row must have one flower with dark petals and one with dark leaves.

Section 5

Eg. 1. b

S stands for a white square and Q for a checked square.

Eg. 2. a

The first and third shape both start with H so H must be the code for shading. The second letter is different for each shape so the second letter must be the code for shape.

P1. c

Square = Y, dark centre = E: YE

P2. c

Sideways triangle = F, dark interior = P: FP

1. d

Upright trapezium = B, inside shape = U: BU

2. c

Dark shapes = S, 2 triangles = E: SE

3. c

GHS = A, sail on the right = S, no top pennant = Z: ASZ

4. e

Left dark triangle = L, top light triangle = W, arrow pointing to RHS = T: LWT

5. b

Inside dark flame = G, outside lined flame = C: GC

6. e

Square outside = B, dark inside shape = F, 1 squiggle = O: BFO

7. c

2 lines = U, small light square = E, position of x on x-axis = W: UEW

8. c

Arrow pointing to the right = H, dark arrow = M: HM

9. a

Top dark bar = D, 2 vertical lines on the right = M: DM

10. c

Two small squares = F, four crosses = E: FE

11. a

3 balls on top = R, arrow at angle = M: RM

12. a

Rectangle on top = R, bar to RHS = L, angled bar on LHS = C: RLC

Practice Test B Answers and Explanations

Section 1

Eg. b

Same shape rotated 45° with dotted side.

P1. d

Shape is inverted.

P2. a

Shape is turned with the shading reversed.

1. d

Inside shape is repeated 3 times: top light, middle horizontal striped, bottom dark.

2. d

Shape turns 90° clockwise and is reflected.

3. e

Half of the original shape with horizontal lines, vertical line, and curved top line.

4. c

Curved lines are straightened and the 3 dark shapes change to match the new shape.

5. c

Shape turns 90° clockwise. Top and middle shape change between light and dark, but the bottom stays the same.

6. b

Reflection with shapes changing between light and dark, and the bottom shape is erased.

7. d

5 lines pinched together at the right.

8. c

Shape reflected with solid sides, then enlarged with dotted sides.

9. e

2 parts slotted together to make a hexagon.

10. b

The small shape multiplies so there is one in each corner and becomes the opposite shading.

11. b

Inverted shape given 2 'feet' and a top circle.

12. b

Small squares become dots, top = double original bottom, bottom = double original top.

Section 2

Eg. c

Right shape is the same as the left but has diagonal lines.

P1. d

Right shape is left shape turned 90°.

P2. c

Right shape is the same as the left, but the inner layer goes from dark to light and the middle layer goes from light to dark.

P3. e

Each corner box has the same pattern.

P4. b

Each row and each column has one of the 3 shapes.

1. d

Larger square remains in the bottom left corner of each box in the bottom row, and the small-large square combination appears once in each row.

2. b

Follow pattern using symmetry: X remains in the bottom right corner, 'eyes' looking down go in

the bottom left corner and top right corner, and the line across the top left corner matches adjoining square.

3. b

Dark shapes change to light, and the box is reflected with 2 horizontal lines.

4. b

Complete squares in top and bottom left corners, and there is a reflection of the triangles in the middle row left square.

5. c

Middle row has medium-sized shapes and each row has a circle, square and triangle.

6. d

Line through the square is removed in the right box, and the shape in the diagonal box is inverted and has horizontal lines added.

7. e

Dark centre shape changes between heart and circle, and arrows point outwards in the boxes on the right. The shapes get smaller on the right.

8. c

Corner shape is the same by column, but in the same position by row, and the main shapes in diagonal boxes are reflected and inverted.

9. c

Same shape in each left box, each shape opens out further along the row.

10. e

Each is the same as the box one down and one left.

11. b

Right boxes have the same shapes as the left, but with 2 short lines at the bottom and a dark rectangle at top point.

12. a

Moving clockwise from the top left box, the shapes rotate 90° clockwise, and each shape gains an additional dark triangle.

Section 3

Eg. 1. b

S stands for a white square and Q for a checked square.

Eg. 2. a

The first and third shape both start with H so H must be the code for shading. The second letter is different for each shape so the second letter must be the code for shape.

P1. c

Square = Y, dark centre = E: YE

P2. c

Sideways triangle = F, dark interior = P: FP

1. a

No dark triangle = Q, circle = S: QS

2 c

Triangles = F, vertical lines = B: FB

3. b

2 vertical dots = W, no connecting shape = O: WO

4. e

Top semicircle = E, 2 arrows = S: ES

5. b

Small square = M, light triangles = F: MF

6. a
   Upright triangle = G, inside shape = F: GF
7. b
   Square = E, small dark square = N,
   dark semicircles = T: ENT
8. a
   Light notes = B, 3 notes = T: BT
9. d
   S shape on side = T, 3 short lines = L: TL
10. a
   Bottom straight line = T, top straight line = P,
   3 crosses on LHS = J: TPJ
11. d
   Dark triangle on LHS = F, light flag on top = R,
   dark triangle on RHS = Z: FRZ
12. b
   Lines top right and bottom left = Y,
   dark triangles = W, dark spots = U: YWU

Section 4

Eg. b
   Square is placed around the X, then in the next box
   the X extends, then another square is placed around
   the extended X, and so on.
P1. a
   New arrow added each time, going in the opposite
   direction to the previously added arrow.
P2. e
   Top V inverts each time, and the line that is bold
   alternates in each box.
1. d
   Dark bottom rectangles in each box, horizontal lines
   increase by 1 each time, dark shape in left corner in
   alternate boxes.
2. c
   Flower pot with flowers increasing by 1 each time,
   light corner shape moves clockwise with original
   becoming dark
3. a
   Use symmetry: fourth section is a reflection of second
   section, fifth section is a reflection of the first section.
4. d
   Central shape rotates 90° clockwise each time, and the
   bottom corner triangle remains in the same place.
5. e
   Each box gains a triangle, triangles on the right side
   of the line are dark, and on the left side are clear. The
   position of the circle in the second half of the sequence
   is a reflection of its position in the first half.
6. c
   Box moves 90° each time, within the box the dark
   squares increase by 1 each time, and single square
   alternates between light and dark.
7. b
   Small arrow moves clockwise around the edge of the
   square, the outside shapes alternate between dark and
   clear, and the outside shapes are circles in the middle
   three boxes, and squares in the outside boxes.
8. e
   Wing lines increase by 1 each time, tail triangles
   increase by 1 each time.
9. d
   Centre dots alternate light and dark, central squares
   alternate large and small, and striped triangle moves
   clockwise round central square.

10. d
   Bottom left square alternates between clear and dark.
   The lines in the bottom left corner increase then
   decrease. Top left string of squares gains an extra
   square in each box, these extra squares come as dark
   and clear alternately.
11. c
   Clear square moves from top left, to middle, to bottom
   right then back to middle and then back to top left.
   Squares coming from the top right increase by one
   each time. Small dark circle alternates between top and
   bottom.
12. a
   Triangle increases in size each time, and squares in the
   top corners alternate in colour.

Section 5

Eg. d
   Quadrilateral with only right angles.
P1. d
   Right-angled triangles.
P2. e
   Small dark right-angled triangle inside each shape.
P3. e
   One small x inside each shape.
1. c
   Each shape has dots on the centre line.
2. d
   Each shape has two small, dark shapes and an open
   symmetrical shape at the top.
3. e
   Each shape has a dotted line of symmetry.
4. d
   All corners of each inner shape must touch the edge of
   the circle.
5. b
   Dark circle, clear triangle, semi-circular base and
   curved top.
6. c
   Each shape consists of two congruent triangles,
   meeting to make a quadrilateral.
7. e
   Symbols either side of the dashed line are symmetrical
   except for the dark squares at the edge.
8. e
   Each shape has a dark square inside.
9. d
   3 shapes intersecting at one corner.
10. b
   Each shape has 2 interior shapes, one clear, one half
   and half.
11. d
   Each shape has three triangles pointing into the same
   corner.
12. a
   Each shape has 2 equal parallel lines with a dark dot
   in the middle.

Practice Test C Answers and Explanations

Section 1

Eg. b
Square is placed around the X, then in the next box the X extends, then another square is placed around the extended X, and so on.

P1. a
New arrow added each time, going in the opposite direction to the previously added arrow.

P2. e
Top V inverts each time, and the line that is bold alternates in each box.

1. b
Eyelashes increase by 1 each time, and iris changes between dark and clear in alternate boxes.

2. d
The pattern is symmetrical, the second box is a reflection of the fourth. Note that the arrowhead in option b is different.

3. a
Line of squares in the top left increases by 1 in each box, and the line of squares in bottom left decreases by 1. Remaining square alternates between top and bottom.

4. e
Shapes move clockwise in each box. Central shape is symmetrical about centre box.

5. c
Triangles rotate 90° anticlockwise in every other box, the small line moves from the left to the middle, then to the right, and then starts again, and the small black square is in alternate boxes.

6. a
Lines with dark circles increase by 1 and the circles become clear, clear circles rotate clockwise by 45°.

7. b
Third pattern is $\frac{1}{2}$ of the first pattern, and the fourth pattern is $\frac{1}{2}$ of the second pattern.

8. c
Small dots moves clockwise round the box, none of the boxes are coloured.

9. d
Corner squares increase in size around the central square, and the shading in the small squares matches that of the larger square in the previous box.

10. e
Shape gains an arm in each box as it rotates clockwise, and once complete gains a small dark dot on the end of the final arm. It then loses an arm in each box.

11. e
Dot and arrow move round edge to middle of RH side and bottom LH corner, arm extended each time. Arms of the cross extend in each box. The black dot moves clockwise and the arrow moves anticlockwise.

12. b
Pattern by alternate boxes, first and fifth boxes match, as the top left flag becomes clear and the lines on the right flag swap sides in the third box, and then revert back in the fifth. Second and fourth boxes are the same.

Section 2

Eg. c
Right shape is the same as the left but has diagonal lines.

P1. d
Right shape is left shape turned 90°.

P2. c
Right shape is the same as the left, but the inner layer goes from dark to light and the middle layer goes from light to dark.

P3. e
Each corner box has the same pattern.

P4. b
Each row and each column has one of the 3 shapes.

1. a
Squares around the central square must have symmetry within, and the square in each corner box must match that in the diagonal corner from it.

2. d
Shapes on the left are the same as the one diagonally across, with the cross only reaching as far as the outer shape and the inner shape removed.

3. b
Each row must have one blank shape, and each row has the same shape that appears in each box within that row. Note that c is too small.

4. b
The ends of the lines in the left box are joined to make the shape in the right box, and the internal lines are removed.

5. c
Right corner boxes must be the same. Divide sign is in the top right of each of the top boxes, equals sign is in the bottom left of each of the bottom boxes.

6. a
Hash symbol is in the top right of each corner box, the musical notes in the left column lose a horizontal line going up in each box.

7. a
Each shape in the right-hand box is a smaller simple version of each shape on the left.

8. a
Dark shape on the left remains the same in the right, and is rotated 45° anticlockwise.

9. d
Shape on the left made 3D on the right.

10. d
Boxes on the right hold the same shape as the boxes on the left, but with a smaller version of the same shape in the same corner as the dark shape in the middle box.

11. a
Umbrella on the right added to the lines in the left boxes. Note that the lines on the bottom of the umbrella are curved not straight.

12. a
Each symbol is the same going diagonally down and right.

Section 3

Eg. b
Same shape rotated 45° with dotted sides.

P1. d
Shape is inverted.

P2. a
Shape is turned with the shading reversed.

1. c

   2 J-shaped lines equal 1 bicycle, therefore 4 J-shaped lines equal 2.

2. d

   Left shape is $\frac{1}{4}$ of the right shape with a dark centre and dotted lines.

3. b

   Right shape is a reflected version of left, with the same markings as the first pair.

4. e

   Shape repeated with cross-hatching, surrounded by a larger similar shape.

5. d

   Shape is inverted, inside line becomes a full shape, and 2 stepped lines are replaced with 3 arrows.

6. e

   Shape turns 90° clockwise, small shapes change shading and the larger shape becomes a shape with the same number of sides as there are smaller shapes.

7. a

   Left top shape is repeated in bottom right corner, right top lines are turned 90°, and bottom left shape is made up of both pairs of lines.

8. c

   Left shape is reflected, changing from dark to light or light to dark, attached by small circle. The straight lines become wavy.

9. a

   Whole shape is stretched to the right, and smaller shapes change from dark to light or light to dark.

10. d

    Inside shapes turn from dark to light or light to dark, and the top of the shape becomes the opposite of curved or straight.

11. a

    Shape is repeated twice, dots change light to dark or dark to light. The top and bottom shapes are the same, and the middle shape has horizontal lines.

12. b

    Shape is inverted, squiggle from top goes right, 2 dark dots go to the top and become light, and a dark rectangle at the bottom edge is added.

Section 4

Eg. 1. b

   The top letter is for the shape, the lower letter is for the type of shading, Q is for square and P for checked. So the code for the checked square is QP.

Eg. 2. c

   The top letter is for the shape, a rectangle is code B and a circle is code C. In each of the three shapes given, there is a different code for the second letter, so this letter must be linked with the pattern inside the shape. One cross is code X so the given pattern is code CX.

P1. a

   Design of triangle = C, orientation of triangle = N: CN

P2. d

   Shape has curve = C, dark inside = B: CB

P3. c

   Square = H, single shape = K: HK

1. c

   No shading = N, light top = Y: NY

2. a

   Triangles = T, dark shapes = S : TS

3. d

   Arrow on bottom = N, one line = U : NU

4. e

   No line through centre = P, shape = G : PG

5. b

   Top LH corner = E, inside shape = A : EA

6. c

   Eyes = R, dark ellipse = C : RC

7. a

   Dark tip = N, hanging shape = A : NA

8. d

   Same triangles = V, corner shape = O : VO

9. c

   Inside design = I, outline = Y : IY

10. d

    Dark shapes = N, dots = E : NE

11. e

    Small dark square at bottom = L, 3 lines from RHS = M : LM

12. a

    Lines in middle = B, curved diagonal lines = Z : BZ

Section 5

Eg. c

   The shapes all have straight sides except for c.

P1. d

   Only dark shape.

P2. c

   Only light arrow.

1. c

   It is the only 'd', all the others are a 'b'.

2. e

   Has a different end to the bisecting line.

3. c

   Chimney is on the left not the right.

4. d

   Bottom squiggle is reversed.

5. c

   More shapes at the top than the bottom.

6. a

   Square is dark instead of light and triangle is light instead of dark.

7. e

   Line does not go through small square at the end.

8. d

   Ends of arms are squares/rhombi not lines.

9. c

   No horizontal lines on the flag.

10. a

    Tail fin has no dark shapes and only four windows when the rest have five.

11. b

    The shape has only one diagonal line from its sides.

12. e

    Odd number of shapes inside.

Practice Test D Answers and Explanations

Section 1

Eg. c

Right shape is the same as the left but has diagonal lines.

P1. d

Right shape is left shape turned 90°

P2. c

Right shape is the same as the left, but the inner layer goes from dark to light and the middle layer goes from light to dark.

P3. e

Each corner box has the same pattern.

P4. b

Each row and each column has one of the 3 shapes.

1. c

Moving from left to right, the large shape rotates 45° and the smaller shape changes from light to dark or dark to light.

2. d

Curved line moves diagonally upwards across the middle row, and the diamond moves diagonally down.

3. a

Moving left to right, circles change to squares and squares change to circles. On the left the small shapes are dark and the lines are outside the shape.

4. e

Same shape in boxes going diagonally up and right.

5. b

Left shape is reduced and placed either side of a central axis with a V at the top.

6. c

Letters are styled by column.

7. b

Left shape is the centre and top lines of the right shape.

8. d

Going from left to right, the line stays the same, but the shapes are doubled and made smaller.

9. d

Snowman is clear, using only the shape on the right.

10. e

Line on the outer shape is on the bottom in each box on the bottom row, and each row must have one of each of the inner shapes.

11. d

Clear dot on the left means 4 clear dots on the right, and the long edge of the shape on the left makes a quarter of the outer shape on the right. There is no rotation involved.

12. d

Middle box contains letter from the left box rotated 180°.

Section 2

Eg. b

Same shape rotated 45° with dotted sides.

P1. d

Shape is inverted.

P2. a

Shape is turned with the shading reversed.

1. d

Shape now has equal sides and smaller, coloured version appears in the centre.

2. b

Shape reflected, and interior has shaded triangles inserted.

3. c

Shape inverted, and the same shape is added to each side, whilst the dot remains in centre.

4. d

Lines of the shape become dotted.

5. e

Shape turns 180°. Note that the shading on a is in the wrong direction.

6. e

Shape is reflected, and final part becomes dark.

7. d

Shape is stretched downwards and has a central vertical line added. The top of the shape forms a V.

8. c

Only intersecting lines remain.

9. e

Shape remains the same except that the outermost arrow on each arm is reversed.

10. c

Dark dot replaced by 3 horizontal lines, and 2 additional lines on central line making 3 in total.

11. a

Shape turns 90°, white bands become shaded, and patterns are reversed.

12. e

Second shape has 4 original shapes attached.

Section 3

Eg. b

Square is placed around the X, then in the next box the X extends, then another square is placed around the extended X, and so on.

P1. a

New arrow added each time, going in the opposite direction to the previously added arrow.

P2. e

Top V inverts each time, and the line that is bold alternates in each box.

1. c

Moving clockwise, a line of the triangle is added until the triangle is complete, then lines are removed.

2. a

Arrow rotates 135° anticlockwise each time.

3. b

Third line is opened out ready to make a square.

4. e

Each box gains a new cross, and a new line going from the centre to the cross that was added in the previous box.

5. d

Heart gets large twice and then smaller twice. The arrow moves clockwise round the box every other box moving from the corner to the centre of the outer line.

6. b

Line is added in one box, then the additional arrow heads are added in the next box.

7. b

Additional arm is added, not intersecting the central circle, and the line in the top left box moves around 45°.

8. **d**
    Number of dots at the top goes up by 1 each time, and number of sides in the central symmetrical shape goes up by 1 each time. The sides of the shape stay the same length. Bottom left small square alternates between light and dark.

9. **a**
    Dark flags increase by 1 each time, blades of grass decrease by 2 each time.

10. **e**
    Starting from the bottom, one arm moves 90° anticlockwise each time, small square is moving round the corners clockwise each time. The short lines change direction one at a time from the bottom up.

11. **c**
    Main shape rotates 90° each time, and an outside dash is lost each time. Note that the internal shape stays the same.

12. **c**
    next arrow added clockwise, centre lines rotate anticlockwise

Section 4

Eg. c
The shapes all have straight sides except for c.

P1. d
Only dark shape.

P2. c
Only light arrow.

1. **b**
    only letter with a curved line.

2. **e**
    All letters have one line of symmetry except Z.

3. **d**
    Inside shape is the only one with 3 sides not 4.

4. **a**
    Lines do not meet at the centre in a.

5. **a**
    Only dark arrow.

6. **b**
    Only pattern with 5 shapes on the horizontal line.

7. **a**
    2 inside lines do not match.

8. **e**
    Number of inside shapes is $\frac{5}{4}$, not equal as other patterns.

9. **b**
    Clock is showing the half-hour not the hour.

10. **c**
    The dark dot is sitting in the outermost corner, not the clear one.

11. **d**
    Has two solid borders not dotted as others. Dot is at base of triangle instead of at apex.

12. **e**
    Dark shape is in the corner not the centre as the others.

Section 5

Eg. 1. b
The top letter is for the shape, the lower letter is for the type of shading, Q is for square and P for checked. So the code for the checked square is QP.

Eg. 2. c
The top letter is for the shape, a rectangle is code B and a circle is code C. In each of the three shapes given, there is a different code for the second letter, so this letter must be linked with the pattern inside the shape. One cross is code X so the given pattern is code CX.

P1. a
Design of triangle = C, orientation of triangle = N: CN

P2. d
Shape has curve = C, dark inside = B: CB

P3. c
Square = H, single shape = K: HK

1. **a**
    Three horizontal lines = R, larger triangle at top = B: RB

2. **d**
    Two small crosses in top left corner = H, dark dot at top = M: HM

3. **b**
    Spade pointing to top left = Y, spade pointing left = O: YO

4. **b**
    Diamond shape = B, overlapping vertical shapes = K: BK

5. **e**
    External shape at RH side = U, external shape is triangle = V: UV

6. **c**
    Horizontal shapes = M, diamonds = P: MP

7. **b**
    3 crosses = L, curve in corner = D: LD

8. **a**
    Small kite in centre = Z, heading has lines and arrow upwards on right = B: ZB

9. **c**
    Border = F, pattern = R: FR

10. **e**
    Second digit 8 = L, first digit 9 = N: LN

11. **d**
    No shape at top left = T, light diamond = B: TB

12. **b**
    Five inside shapes = K, inside shapes are triangles = N: KN

Notes

Notes

Notes

NON-VERBAL REASONING TEST A

Pupil's Name		

School Name		

PUPIL NUMBER

[0]	[0]	[0]	[0]	[0]	[0]
[1]	[1]	[1]	[1]	[1]	[1]
[2]	[2]	[2]	[2]	[2]	[2]
[3]	[3]	[3]	[3]	[3]	[3]
[4]	[4]	[4]	[4]	[4]	[4]
[5]	[5]	[5]	[5]	[5]	[5]
[6]	[6]	[6]	[6]	[6]	[6]
[7]	[7]	[7]	[7]	[7]	[7]
[8]	[8]	[8]	[8]	[8]	[8]
[9]	[9]	[9]	[9]	[9]	[9]

SCHOOL NUMBER

[0]	[0]	[0]	[0]	[0]	[0]	[0]
[1]	[1]	[1]	[1]	[1]	[1]	[1]
[2]	[2]	[2]	[2]	[2]	[2]	[2]
[3]	[3]	[3]	[3]	[3]	[3]	[3]
[4]	[4]	[4]	[4]	[4]	[4]	[4]
[5]	[5]	[5]	[5]	[5]	[5]	[5]
[6]	[6]	[6]	[6]	[6]	[6]	[6]
[7]	[7]	[7]	[7]	[7]	[7]	[7]
[8]	[8]	[8]	[8]	[8]	[8]	[8]
[9]	[9]	[9]	[9]	[9]	[9]	[9]

DATE OF BIRTH

Day		Month		Year	
[0]	[0]	January	☐	1990	☐
[1]	[1]	February	☐	1991	☐
[2]	[2]	March	☐	1992	☐
[3]	[3]	April	☐	1993	☐
	[4]	May	☐	1994	☐
	[5]	June	☐	1995	☐
	[6]	July	☐	1996	☐
	[7]	August	☐	1997	☐
	[8]	September	☐	1998	☐
	[9]	October	☐	1999	☐
		November	☐	2000	☐
		December	☐	2001	☐

Please mark like this ⊢.

SECTION 1

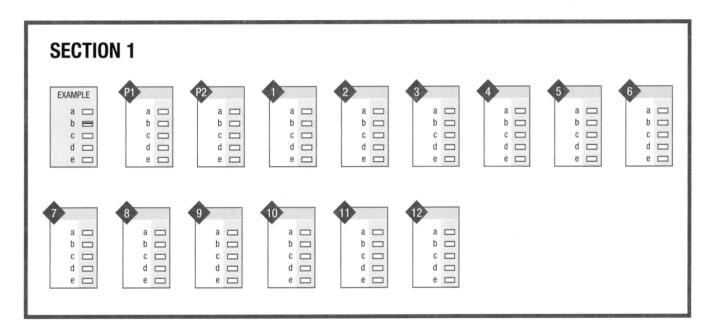

SECTION 2

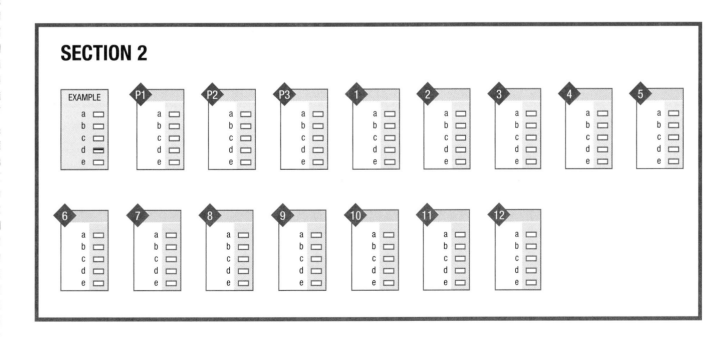

PUPIL NUMBER

[0]	[0]	[0]	[0]	[0]	[0]
[1]	[1]	[1]	[1]	[1]	[1]
[2]	[2]	[2]	[2]	[2]	[2]
[3]	[3]	[3]	[3]	[3]	[3]
[4]	[4]	[4]	[4]	[4]	[4]
[5]	[5]	[5]	[5]	[5]	[5]
[6]	[6]	[6]	[6]	[6]	[6]
[7]	[7]	[7]	[7]	[7]	[7]
[8]	[8]	[8]	[8]	[8]	[8]
[9]	[9]	[9]	[9]	[9]	[9]

SECTION 3

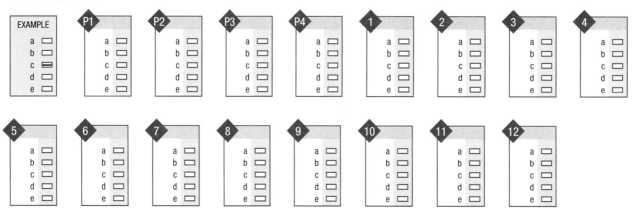

SECTION 4

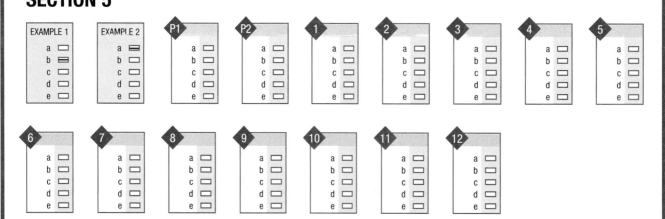

SECTION 5

Pupil's Name

School Name

Date of Test

DATE OF BIRTH

Day	Month	Year

Please mark like this ⊟.

PUPIL NUMBER

[0] [0] [0] [0] [0] [0]
[1] [1] [1] [1] [1] [1]
[2] [2] [2] [2] [2] [2]
[3] [3] [3] [3] [3] [3]
[4] [4] [4] [4] [4] [4]
[5] [5] [5] [5] [5] [5]
[6] [6] [6] [6] [6] [6]
[7] [7] [7] [7] [7] [7]
[8] [8] [8] [8] [8] [8]
[9] [9] [9] [9] [9] [9]

SCHOOL NUMBER

[0] [0] [0] [0] [0] [0] [0]
[1] [1] [1] [1] [1] [1] [1]
[2] [2] [2] [2] [2] [2] [2]
[3] [3] [3] [3] [3] [3] [3]
[4] [4] [4] [4] [4] [4] [4]
[5] [5] [5] [5] [5] [5] [5]
[6] [6] [6] [6] [6] [6] [6]
[7] [7] [7] [7] [7] [7] [7]
[8] [8] [8] [8] [8] [8] [8]
[9] [9] [9] [9] [9] [9] [9]

[0] [0]	January ▭	1990 ▭
[1] [1]	February ▭	1991 ▭
[2] [2]	March ▭	1992 ▭
[3] [3]	April ▭	1993 ▭
[4]	May ▭	1994 ▭
[5]	June ▭	1995 ▭
[6]	July ▭	1996 ▭
[7]	August ▭	1997 ▭
[8]	September ▭	1998 ▭
[9]	October ▭	1999 ▭
	November ▭	2000 ▭
	December ▭	2001 ▭

SECTION 1

SECTION 2

    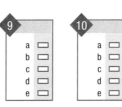  

PUPIL NUMBER

[0]	[0]	[0]	[0]	[0]	[0]
[1]	[1]	[1]	[1]	[1]	[1]
[2]	[2]	[2]	[2]	[2]	[2]
[3]	[3]	[3]	[3]	[3]	[3]
[4]	[4]	[4]	[4]	[4]	[4]
[5]	[5]	[5]	[5]	[5]	[5]
[6]	[6]	[6]	[6]	[6]	[6]
[7]	[7]	[7]	[7]	[7]	[7]
[8]	[8]	[8]	[8]	[8]	[8]
[9]	[9]	[9]	[9]	[9]	[9]

SECTION 3

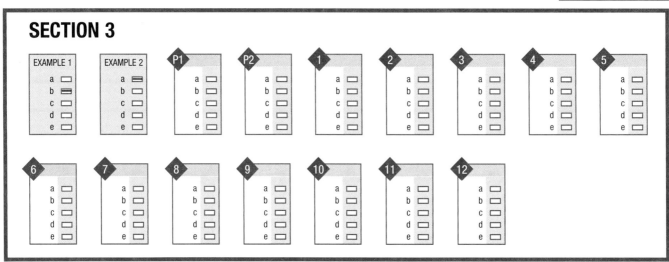

SECTION 4

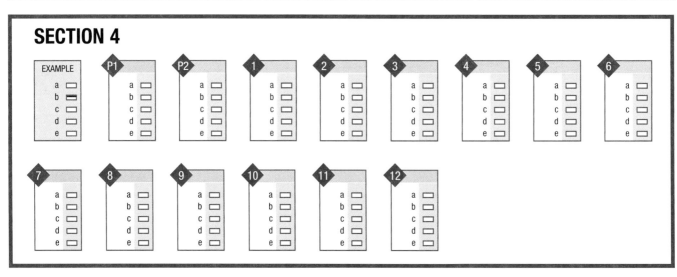

SECTION 5

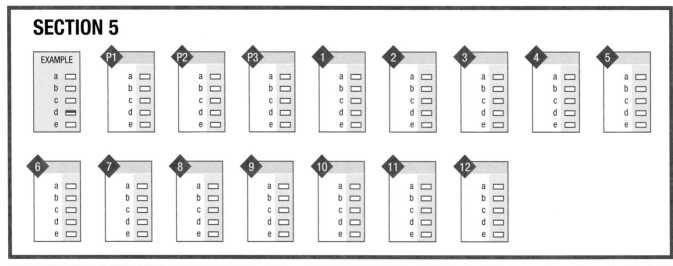

Pupil's Name

School Name

© Letts Educational Ltd

Date of Test

DATE OF BIRTH

Day	Month		Year	
[0] [0]	January	☐	1990	☐
[1] [1]	February	☐	1991	☐
[2] [2]	March	☐	1992	☐
[3] [3]	April	☐	1993	☐
[4]	May	☐	1994	☐
[5]	June	☐	1995	☐
[6]	July	☐	1996	☐
[7]	August	☐	1997	☐
[8]	September	☐	1998	☐
[9]	October	☐	1999	☐
	November	☐	2000	☐
	December	☐	2001	☐

PUPIL NUMBER

[0]	[0]	[0]	[0]	[0]	[0]
[1]	[1]	[1]	[1]	[1]	[1]
[2]	[2]	[2]	[2]	[2]	[2]
[3]	[3]	[3]	[3]	[3]	[3]
[4]	[4]	[4]	[4]	[4]	[4]
[5]	[5]	[5]	[5]	[5]	[5]
[6]	[6]	[6]	[6]	[6]	[6]
[7]	[7]	[7]	[7]	[7]	[7]
[8]	[8]	[8]	[8]	[8]	[8]
[9]	[9]	[9]	[9]	[9]	[9]

SCHOOL NUMBER

[0]	[0]	[0]	[0]	[0]	[0]	[0]
[1]	[1]	[1]	[1]	[1]	[1]	[1]
[2]	[2]	[2]	[2]	[2]	[2]	[2]
[3]	[3]	[3]	[3]	[3]	[3]	[3]
[4]	[4]	[4]	[4]	[4]	[4]	[4]
[5]	[5]	[5]	[5]	[5]	[5]	[5]
[6]	[6]	[6]	[6]	[6]	[6]	[6]
[7]	[7]	[7]	[7]	[7]	[7]	[7]
[8]	[8]	[8]	[8]	[8]	[8]	[8]
[9]	[9]	[9]	[9]	[9]	[9]	[9]

Please mark like this ⊟.

SECTION 1

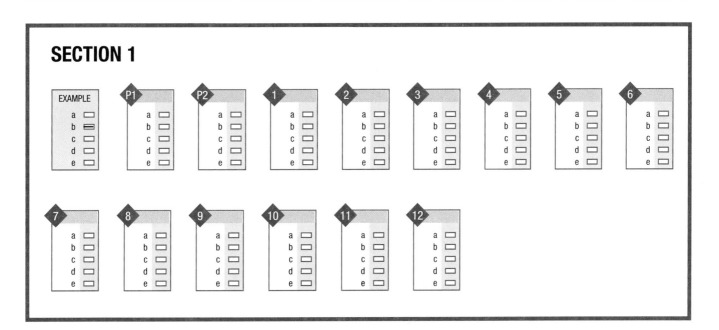

SECTION 2

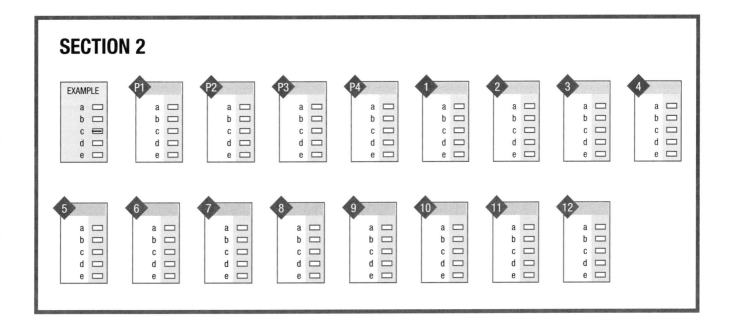

PUPIL NUMBER

[0]	[0]	[0]	[0]	[0]	[0]
[1]	[1]	[1]	[1]	[1]	[1]
[2]	[2]	[2]	[2]	[2]	[2]
[3]	[3]	[3]	[3]	[3]	[3]
[4]	[4]	[4]	[4]	[4]	[4]
[5]	[5]	[5]	[5]	[5]	[5]
[6]	[6]	[6]	[6]	[6]	[6]
[7]	[7]	[7]	[7]	[7]	[7]
[8]	[8]	[8]	[8]	[8]	[8]
[9]	[9]	[9]	[9]	[9]	[9]

SECTION 3

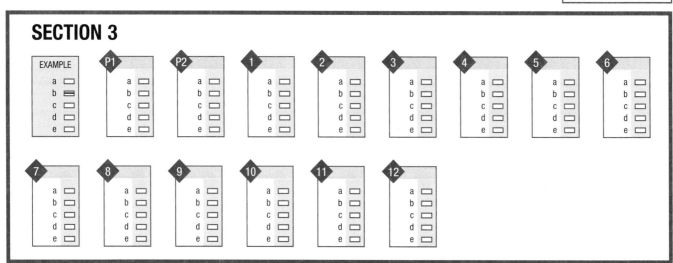

SECTION 4

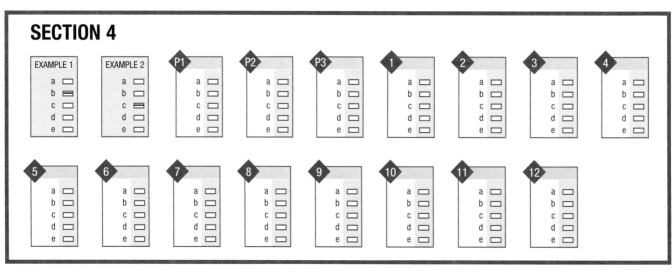

SECTION 5

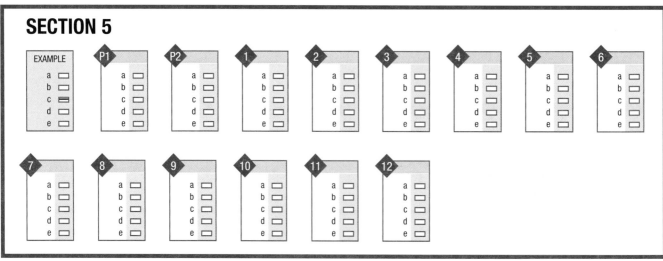

NON-VERBAL REASONING TEST D

NVR D

Pupil's Name

School Name

Date of Test

DATE OF BIRTH

Day		Month		Year	
[0]	[0]	January	▭	1990	▭
[1]	[1]	February	▭	1991	▭
[2]	[2]	March	▭	1992	▭
[3]	[3]	April	▭	1993	▭
	[4]	May	▭	1994	▭
	[5]	June	▭	1995	▭
	[6]	July	▭	1996	▭
	[7]	August	▭	1997	▭
	[8]	September	▭	1998	▭
	[9]	October	▭	1999	▭
		November	▭	2000	▭
		December	▭	2001	▭

PUPIL NUMBER

[0]	[0]	[0]	[0]	[0]	[0]
[1]	[1]	[1]	[1]	[1]	[1]
[2]	[2]	[2]	[2]	[2]	[2]
[3]	[3]	[3]	[3]	[3]	[3]
[4]	[4]	[4]	[4]	[4]	[4]
[5]	[5]	[5]	[5]	[5]	[5]
[6]	[6]	[6]	[6]	[6]	[6]
[7]	[7]	[7]	[7]	[7]	[7]
[8]	[8]	[8]	[8]	[8]	[8]
[9]	[9]	[9]	[9]	[9]	[9]

SCHOOL NUMBER

[0]	[0]	[0]	[0]	[0]	[0]	[0]
[1]	[1]	[1]	[1]	[1]	[1]	[1]
[2]	[2]	[2]	[2]	[2]	[2]	[2]
[3]	[3]	[3]	[3]	[3]	[3]	[3]
[4]	[4]	[4]	[4]	[4]	[4]	[4]
[5]	[5]	[5]	[5]	[5]	[5]	[5]
[6]	[6]	[6]	[6]	[6]	[6]	[6]
[7]	[7]	[7]	[7]	[7]	[7]	[7]
[8]	[8]	[8]	[8]	[8]	[8]	[8]
[9]	[9]	[9]	[9]	[9]	[9]	[9]

Please mark like this ⊢.

SECTION 1

EXAMPLE a, b, c, d, e — P1, P2, P3, P4, 1, 2, 3, 4

5, 6, 7, 8, 9, 10, 11, 12

SECTION 2

EXAMPLE a, b, c, d, e — P1, P2, 1, 2, 3, 4, 5, 6

7, 8, 9, 10, 11, 12

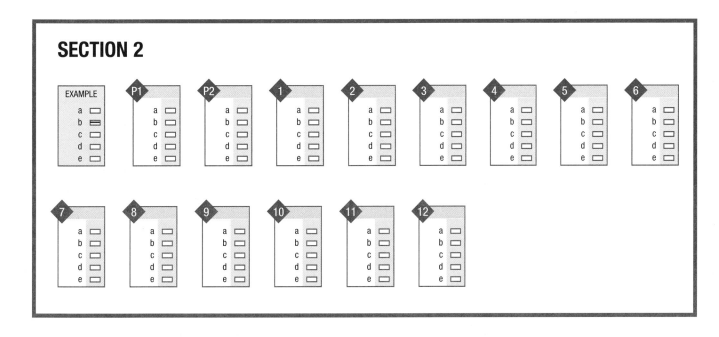

PUPIL NUMBER

[0]	[0]	[0]	[0]	[0]	[0]
[1]	[1]	[1]	[1]	[1]	[1]
[2]	[2]	[2]	[2]	[2]	[2]
[3]	[3]	[3]	[3]	[3]	[3]
[4]	[4]	[4]	[4]	[4]	[4]
[5]	[5]	[5]	[5]	[5]	[5]
[6]	[6]	[6]	[6]	[6]	[6]
[7]	[7]	[7]	[7]	[7]	[7]
[8]	[8]	[8]	[8]	[8]	[8]
[9]	[9]	[9]	[9]	[9]	[9]

SECTION 3

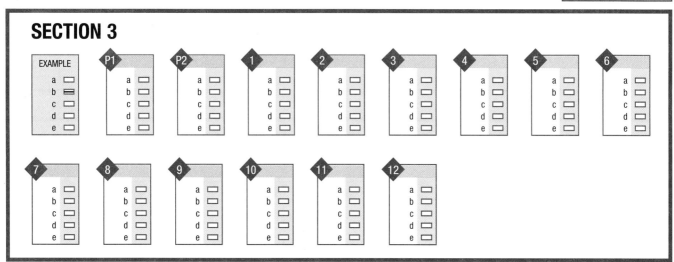

SECTION 4

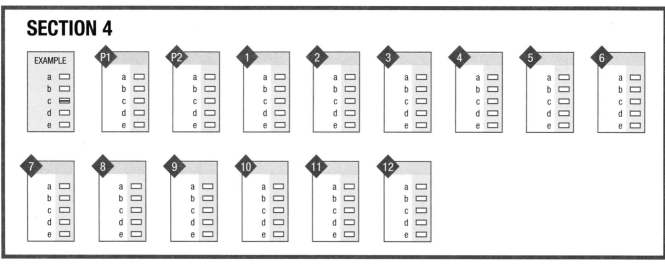

SECTION 5

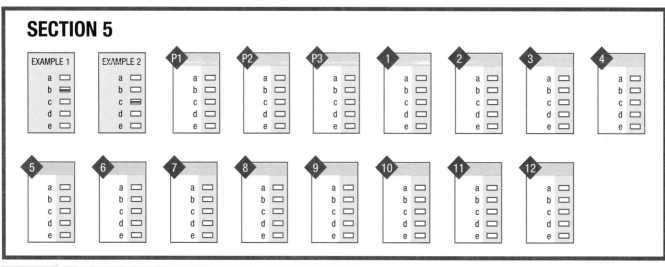